PLAYING FOR THE CITY

THE POWER OF SPORTS FOR CHRISTIAN COMMUNITY DEVELOPMENT

Jeff Biddle, Jr.
James "Jamie" Jessup
Chris Lahr
Jeff Thompson

Urban Loft Publishers | Skyforest, CA

“Rooted in the principles and historical stories of Christian community development, authors Biddle, Jessup, Lahr, & Thompson bring their personal insights and experiences and lay a foundation for their readers that is holistic and forward thinking. By sharing how they intentionally shape, protect, guide and empower athletes, their communities and racial structures, no stone is left unturned. I highly recommend this book as it is an honest, deep dive into the many facets of building equitable communities through sports programming.”

MICHELLE FERRIGNO WARREN
Activist & Author, *The Power of Proximity: Moving Beyond Awareness to Action*

"Much that gets written concerning the efficacy of "sports and the city" reads either dismissively (through the lens of capitalistic failures) or shortsightedly (viewed simply as a path to character development.) *Playing for the City* offers a vision at once more hopeful and expansive, one whose ultimate measure of success is dependent on Spirit-filled people rather than simply the flow of dollars or virtuous individuality. It provides an argument for a comprehensive approach to human and community development through sports while also offering an opportunity to hear first-person accounts from players, coaches, and leaders from around the country actually experiencing transformation. Part urban missions manual, part leadership textbook, *Playing for the City* equips sports-minded Christians hungry for change with a way forward. It practically shows how in the hands of a few committed Christians ready to love deeply, sports offer a weapon for communal change waiting to be discharged. If God gave you both sports and community as a stewardship, this book is for you!"

DR. ED USZINSKI
Athletes in Action staff, Ph.D., American Cultural Studies

"*Playing for the City* offers a treasure chest of vision, wisdom and practices for parents, coaches, youth workers, local pastors or community organizers who are interested in channeling their passion for sports into activities that will build a better life for the individuals and communities they love."

PAT MCLEOD
Boston Metro Director and Harvard Chaplain, Athletes in Action, Author, *Hit Hard: One Family's Journey of Letting Go of What Was – and Learning to Live Well with What Is*

"Jeff Biddle and his team are among the pioneers in the emerging area of scholarship and leadership examining sport for Christian Community Development. *Playing for the City* integrates the stories of coaches, athletes, administrators, ministers, families, neighbors, and many others to deliver a much-needed framework for harnessing and leveraging the power of sport to empower and transform individuals as well as communities. This book offers a holistic primer on Christocentric, culturally competent strategies to develop sustainable community leadership in and through sport. The sport experience is arguably a microcosm of the way God intended community and the church to be – *Playing for the City* is an inspiring account of how we can steward the gift of sport to be loving neighbors and advocates for justice, peace, reconciliation, and shalom in our communities."

DR. LANDON HUFFMAN
Professor of Sport and Fitness Leadership, Johnson University

"Sports saved my life. Not only my life, but the lives of so many of my friends. God, in a way that only He could orchestrate, has used sports to transform people and communities. I highly recommend *Playing for the City*; in it you will see how sports have been a powerful force in community transformation for decades."

DR. DERWIN L. GRAY
Lead Pastor Transformation Church; Author, *The Good Life: What Jesus Teaches About True Happiness*

Playing for the City: The Power of Sports for Christian Community Development

Write: Permissions, Urban Loft Publishers
PO Box 6
Skyforest, Ca 92385
www.urbanloftpublishers.com

Senior Editors: Stephen Burris & Kendi Howells Douglas
Copy Editor: Christian Arnold
Graphics: Amber Craft

ISBN-13: 978-1-949625-10-3

Made in the United States.

TABLE OF CONTENTS

Foreword

Sports in American culture have become far more than our American pastime. We used to say that baseball was our pastime, but now professional sports have inundated the American culture and have become a huge business. Professional sports have changed the nature of athletics and turned it into more of an entertainment business. Professional athletes make exorbitant salaries and we as consumers continue to support them through television, attendance at stadiums, and buying team jerseys and sports gear, along with the idolization of the stars.

Being a spectator and a fan is what sports have become. But that's not the real sports story. Athletics, in its intent, is an extremely positive activity. It's not the spectator that's significant, but the participant. Youth sports have been extremely valuable in helping young people do very positive things, and have been a wonderful tool to help our youth focus on becoming the person God intended them to be. Sports build character; it's often when adults and when outside forces get involved that the purity of sport is damaged. Millions of young people participate in youth sports through their grammar schools and high schools every day. This has enabled them to stay in school, focus on their education, stay out of trouble with so much idle time, and become better people. How marvelous it is when youth participate in sports and realize the significance of teamwork, hard work, dedication, and fun. Yes—sports are intended to be fun. And whenever they're not fun, we need to take a closer look at what's going on.

My wife Anne and I have spent the last 45 years using sports for community development on the westside of Chicago. We call our philosophy "Christian Community Development." It is based in eight key components of ministry: Relocation, Reconciliation, Redistribution, Leadership Development, Church-Based, Listening to the Community, Wholistic Approach and Empowerment. Together, these components combined with sports activities have had a huge positive impact in North Lawndale on Chicago's westside and hundreds of other under-resourced neighborhoods around the world. We have seen how sports and a love for community can make a difference. In fact, our church and ministry have three gymnasiums, and a fitness center which had over 200,000 participant visits last year. We have several sports teams that compete on multiple levels. Sports is a fabulous resource coupled with Christian Community Development to build strong communities.

This book is getting back to the positives of sports, and how they can build character and community. The authors have worked hard to show how sports can make a difference. I know this firsthand, not only as a high school athlete, but also as a high school coach. It was through the Fellowship of Christian athletes that I committed my life to Jesus Christ while in high school; It was through coaching at Farragut high school in Chicago that a Bible study was started through the Fellowship of Christian athletes. From this small Bible study, Lawndale Community Church was birthed. It was the idea of young people who saw that their community could be better.

These young people understood almost innately that Christianity, sports and community development all went hand-in-hand. If you love the Lord, you love your neighbor. That's the essence of this book: using athletics and Christian Community Development make a difference in communities.

That's why I am so excited about *Playing for the City: The Power of Sports for Christian Community Development* by Jeff Biddle, Jr., James "Jamie" Jessup, Chris Lahr and Jeff Thompson. They combine the principles of Christian Community Development and the important aspects of sports together. They have all been successful in practically living out these principles and using sports and community development as a discipling and character-building source in the lives of young people and those that they touch. This book gives wonderful insights on how to actually do this successfully.

Sports and Community Development can make a major impact on our communities. These are not often placed together, but *Playing for the City* has magnificently shown us how to accomplish these collectively. This book will guide us into doing this great work better.

WAYNE "COACH" GORDON

Introduction

In 2006, Detroit hosted the Super Bowl at Ford Field, home of the Detroit Lions. With the auto industry in steady decline and the population half what it was in mid-century, the industrial boomtown was in an economic tailspin, and the NFL Championship game was expected to bring a much-needed stimulus to the city's businesses. Still, local activists who saw hosting the Superbowl as a short-sighted publicity stunt hung a huge homemade banner from an overpass near downtown:

"SPORTS WON'T SAVE OUR CITY"

We disagree. For America's struggling communities, sports are no mere gimmick or distraction. When approached in the right way, sports have the potential to be the lifeblood of community transformation.

To see one stunning example, take a train west from Detroit, and in four hours you will arrive at Chicago's Union Station. Take a Pink Line "L" train to Pulaski Station and walk a block south through the North Lawndale neighborhood, and you can see what people have called the "Lawndale Miracle."

In the late 1970s, North Lawndale was estimated to be the fifteenth-poorest neighborhood in the United States. But during that time, Coach Wayne Gordon, who had moved to Lawndale from Iowa to teach at Ferragut High School, and fifteen of his high school athletes, were dreaming and praying together about what they might do to make their community stronger. They decided to start by forming a church, and keep going from there (Gordon, 1995).

Today, Lawndale Community Church sits at the center of a network of ministries and businesses that have built a thriving local community. Ogden Avenue is lined with a health center, a legal center, a youth center, and an athletic center. Hundreds of local homes have been renovated and restored, hundreds of young people have gone to college and found work, and many of those have returned to raise their families in Lawndale. Lawndale's civic leaders now advocate for prosperity and justice for those in their neighborhood, their city, and beyond. The entire face of the community has changed—and those who remember how it all began knowing that the transformation started with a group of young athletes and their dream. Sports brought people together in a way that fueled a movement of faith, peace, justice, and prosperity in a whole neighborhood.

How did it happen? It happened when the dreams of youth athletes were given form and power by a philosophy that applied the gospel of Christ to their circumstances.

The Lawndale athletes were much like their peers around the country. Those of us who live, coach, work, or volunteer in under-resourced places know that our young people dream passionately about using their time and talents to lift up those they love, and build a thriving community where people are free to focus on their families, their callings, and the joys of life instead of on how to pay the next bill or stay safe from violence. Many are sure that their passion for sports can contribute to making that dream a reality.

But the dream by itself is not enough—the dream needs to be shaped, protected, guided, and empowered. Too often, we endure the slow tragedy of seeing those dreams ground to dust by vicious cycles of poverty, violence, racism and broken social systems. We ache to know how next time might be different, and we long to see the strength and passion displayed on the athletic field released to breathe life into our beloved communities.

What set North Lawndale apart? How did fifteen athletes and their coach, dreaming together in the midst of one of the most violent neighborhoods in America, spark a transformation that has lasted for forty years?

They didn't work alone. Coach Gordon and the Lawndale athletes had another "coach"—civil rights leader Dr. John Perkins. John was born in Mendenhall, Mississippi, in 1930. After growing up in segregated poverty and watching his war veteran brother gunned down by police, John married and moved to California, where he first found success and security, and then, with the help of one of his young children, found Jesus. He felt called to return as a minister to his native Mendenhall, where the Civil Rights Movement was gaining steam. After leading an economic boycott, John was arrested and tortured by police officers inside a jail. He emerged from the experience convinced that only faith, reconciliation, and economic empowerment could bring the kind of healing that his community—and so many communities—needed (Perkins, 1976). The philosophy Dr. Perkins developed came to be called "Christian Community Development." Christian Community Development, in turn, became the framework that gave structure and strategy to the dreams of Lawndale, and has since empowered ministries—including sports ministries—all over the country.

Can sports be a tool to harness the passions of young people and create lasting, positive change? Absolutely—in many ways, organized sports are designed perfectly for the job. In some neighborhoods, youth sports leagues are the best-organized youth programs in existence, and one of the only places where mature men and young boys interact in a structured way. Athletes are often social leaders in their schools and peer groups, and sports teach emotional regulation and leadership. In neighborhoods where public places can be dangerous, sports teams can be one of the safest outlets for energy and self-expression. School teams are publicly funded and community teams have connections to business sponsors. High school, college, and professional teams inspire a sort of civic pride that crosses nearly every demographic boundary. In North America, sports opens up countless opportunities at educational institutions through scholarships and other programs. The possibilities for community transformation through sports are nearly endless. One of the greatest tools for the development and enrichment of communities across America is sitting right under our noses.

We see it clearly when a successful professional athlete like LeBron James opens the *I Promise* school in his native Akron, using his own success to reinvest in the community that raised him, supporting and inspiring many others in the process. But most young athletes will never "go pro," never make millions, never even make a dime off their athletic career, and their hopes for their own communities are just the same. How do we give power and structure to those hopes? How do we move past the "sports as a way out" trope that has been projected on low-income youth for decades, and focus on building a *way forward* that is far less individualistic, far more realistic, and far more inclusive? How do we use the power of sports to achieve collectively what no one could achieve alone?

It takes more than a Bible verse at halftime or even a scholarship to college—it takes a deliberate, community-based strategy, where people across the boundaries of age, economics, and ethnicity work together in a way that is empowering and enriching for everyone involved. Senators and CEOs will gladly tell how their participation in athletics as young people molded their character and built the foundation for their success. But in order to turn sports into the kind of transformational tool that so many of our young people dream of, we have to move beyond the *character* development that so many successful sports ministries already practice, to a *community-based* approach; we have to leverage the social capital, civic pride, and institutional connections already present in the North American sports world through the transforming power of the gospel of Christ to bring people together and blend their talents in pursuit of love and justice. It can be done. It has been done. That's what this book is all about.

The four of us together have decades of experience using the power of sports to transform our communities.

- JEFF BIDDLE, JR. is a pastor and sports chaplain in Charles-ton, West Virginia, and the founding director of the *Midian Leadership Project*, a sports-based nonprofit. His doctoral research at Palmer Seminary focused on community leader-ship development through sports among boys affected by the school-to-prison pipeline.
- JAMES "JAMIE" JESSUP is a schoolteacher and a football and basketball coach in metropolitan Atlanta, and the founding director of *Camp Clutch,* a community-development-based basketball camp in Winston-Salem, North Carolina.
- CHRIS LAHR is the former general manager of *Timoteo Sports*, a non-profit sports ministry that provides mentorship to youth and young adults in North Philadelphia's Kensington neighborhood.
- JEFF THOMPSON is the founding director of *10:12 Sports*, a nonprofit sports ministry in Baltimore's Sandtown neighborhood, and played Division One football for the University of Delaware.

Maybe you are a youth pastor, a parachurch worker, or a volunteer who has seen the passion that young people have for athletics, and you want to know more about how to harness that passion for Christ in world-transforming ways, ways that touch the rawest wounds and deepest longings of your neighborhood. Maybe you've been in sports ministry for years, or maybe you are looking to start your first season. Either way, this book is for you.

Maybe you are a chaplain, tasked with the spiritual care and uplift of a whole team, some believers, some not, some not sure. Maybe you are looking for a way to connect spiritual truth with the real and present needs and ambitions of the athletes and the community you serve. This book is for you.

Maybe you are a coach from a neighborhood where young people struggle to move forward. Maybe you have invested years in the joys and cares, successes and failures of your own and your neighbors' children, passing on your wisdom and lending your support in whatever way you can. Maybe you have seen the power that sports have to form and transform young people and their futures, and you want to know how to deepen and strengthen that impact in a way that will give substance to hopes and alter the future for you and the people you share life with. This book is for you.

Maybe you are a coach from a middle-class background, coaching athletes whose background is very different from yours, young people who pin so many hopes on their athletic careers, and yet face challenges that are difficult to understand. Maybe you are looking for insight into the hope and the heartbreak, hoping to offer the kind of guidance your young people need. This book is for you.

Maybe you are an athlete, searching for a kind of success with significance beyond the moment of victory, beyond even a college scholarship. Maybe you have realized how people have begun to look up to you, and you don't want to let them down. Maybe you are looking for a way to honor the needs of your family and community and the call of your own journey and future at the same time. Maybe you wonder if that is even possible. It *is* possible, and this book is especially for you.

Maybe somebody put this book in your hands, telling you it contained something you needed to know. We like to think that they are right. This book is for you.

But no matter who you are, if you are reading this, some part of you believes that sports are a powerful ministry tool in under-resourced places, and some part of you wants to be a part of the transformation. Keep reading. You are not alone. Your hope of seeing sports do tangible good for your community is not a pipe dream.

There are models to follow and models still being created that will help you do just that. That stirring feeling that something far deeper, more important, and more lasting than you have yet understood is going on during Friday night football or Saturday morning basketball, that deep sense that the brotherhood and sisterhood forged in the trenches of the game can have a lifelong impact far beyond the field—those feelings are valid. Read on to hear stories that let you know that those hours spent practicing and coaching, shuttling people from home to practice, running jerseys through the laundry, and scheduling gym times can and do make a difference.

Together we will see how sports have been a powerful force in community transformation for decades. We will hear from athletes, coaches, pastors, and teachers who have put their sports passions to work for the sake of the neighborhoods and people they love. We will explore possibilities and models for using the games we love as a chance to apply some of the most successful community development strategies developed in North America. The sports that bring us so much joy, the games that light up young people's faces and draw crowds from all over the city, the joy and energy and passion they unleash, are harnessing a power that, with God's help, can transform the communities we love.

Relocation: Finding Our Home Turf

If you picked up this book, you probably already know that sports are an incredible tool for creating an energetic presence within a community; sports bring neighbors and strangers together for a common purpose, from little league to the Olympic games. Effective community ministry through sports is about harnessing the energy of that *presence.*

John Perkins' philosophy of Christian Community Development is rooted in what he calls the "Three R's": *Relocation, Reconciliation,* and *Redistribution.* The first of these, *Relocation,* is about *presence*: effective community transformation comes with the authentic, intentional, transforming *presence* of God and His people within the community. The idea of a redeeming *presence* comes from the example of Christ himself, who left Heaven for Earth to walk among his people, live a holy life, and sacrifice himself for the salvation of the world. Philippians 2:6-7 teaches that Jesus, "being in very nature God, did not consider equality with God something to be used to his own advantage; rather, he made himself nothing, taking on the very nature of a servant, being made in human likeness." Jesus did not hesitate to spend his time among the poor and the outcast, insisting to those who questioned his motives: "the Son of Man came not to be served, but to serve, and to give his life as a ransom for many" (Matthew 20:28).

Sports: The Solution Right Under Our Noses

Let's take a mental walk through an imaginary yet familiar neighborhood—we'll call it Cross Corners—on a weekday afternoon. Though there are some people moving around between lunch places and other shops, Cross Corners isn't too busy. Boarded windows on brick stores and wood houses show that the neighborhood was built for more people and more business than it has today. People wave cheerfully from porches and talk in doorways, but one can feel from the pace of the place that people are less occupied than they would like to be. The sign on one large church advertises a pastoral anniversary next week; a church just down the street is overgrown with weeds and one of the front rails is broken. The people of Cross Corners are warm and kind, but its glory days are in the past.

Take a watchful walk through the high school, and you may notice the effect that hard times are having on the young people. There are chains reinforcing the locks on certain doors. There are more girls than boys in the halls. Some of the teachers seem stern and almost fearful when they interact with the students. The final bell rings, and a fight breaks out before the buses leave for the surrounding blocks. Most of the students just laugh, recording reactions with their phones and ambling on when the commotion dies down. Few adults seem to notice.

People move around in the afternoon, but as night falls, the streets empty out, except for some groups of young men. They laugh and talk and walk and don't seem to be up to much, but they seem used to people assuming the worst about them; they stop smiling and glance up with apprehension when strangers get close. After dark, the few others in the streets seem not to feel entirely safe, walking more briskly, staying close to buildings, double-checking the locks on their cars. Every once in awhile, a police cruiser hums slowly down the block, then turns without a signal. An airplane passes audibly overhead; the nearby traffic light goes through a whole cycle with no cars passing through. Things are still, but the stillness isn't exactly what one could call peaceful.

Cross Corners could be almost anywhere in North America. It could be a neighborhood in Queens or an old market town in Texas; its people could be White or Black, an immigrant enclave or a multicultural mosaic. Cross Corners could be anywhere that the economy has passed by and the powerful have written off; many of us call such places home, or we once did. But we haven't quite finished our evening walk through Cross Corners. There is one place that is filled with incredible energy.

At the end of our walk, we arrive at a local gymnasium. Or perhaps it is the football field, or the soccer pitch. But here, the lights are bright, and the noise is a joyful roar of laughter and conversation.

Friends and families move together between bleachers, concession stands, and open spaces. Sometimes half the crowd moves all at once: at tense moments, the packs of young men stand to their feet, shoulder-to shoulder with middle-aged women cupping their hands to their mouths to shout as venerable silver-haired grandfathers throw their arms up in the air; these unlikely companions have been drawn into coordinated motion by the gripping scene unfolding below. Here, the energy is pulsing. Here, the young people move with purpose. Here, the generations blend. Here, the fruit of the Spirit—love, joy, peace, and all that go with them—are written on the faces. Here, God is at work, bringing a community together.

In nearly every distressed community in North America, God is *already* doing an amazing work through sports programs—and He has been for generations. Sports are an incredible tool for community development, rooted by their nature in the community itself. Sports teams take their very names from communities—the *Cleveland* Cavaliers, the University of *California* at *Los Angeles* Bruins, the *Huntington North* High School Vikings, The *West Side* Warriors. Some are attached to schools and funded with public money. Some are attached to neighborhoods and funded with corporate sponsorships. Some are attached to churches and funded with gifts. In each case, community resources are packaged and directed toward youth development and community life.

In fact, in many struggling neighborhoods, youth sports are one of the best-organized youth development assets available to families. Especially in places where public spaces may be unsafe, and educational institutions are underfunded or have had their missions corrupted by politically motivated discipline policies, families have been turning to youth sports for years for their children's safe social development. Common sense experience and a host of research teaches us the incredible value of sports in positive youth development and character formation. But it isn't just the athletes who benefit—all over the world, sports harness the passions of the community and bring people together. God is at work in a big way. All we have to do is join in.

Location, Location, Location

To be a *presence,* by definition, we need to be in the right *place.* Location is incredibly important to community ministry; any facility used for community sports needs to be in the right place, especially in under-resourced communities where more people depend on extended family and community resources for transportation. For community-based programs to make a real difference, a location within the community is vital – the program exists for the community, not the community for the program. School sports programs will usually (though not always) be located in community facilities by default, although their condition will depend significantly on the political question what resources have been allocated to the community schools. The right place can be hard to find, but at the end of the day, if we start with the intention of loving and serving our neighbors, the facilities will come with time.

Most communities already have more facilities suited for sports than most people realize. Nearly every school has a gymnasium and at least one outdoor sports field, as do many churches. Bigger cities almost always have a YMCA, a Boys and Girls Club, and other nonprofit activity centers. Old schools which have been converted for other purposes often have underused sports facilities, and community centers and parks run within the neighborhood by the city or county can serve as spaces for all sorts of sports programs. In some places, the right facility might not exist yet—for example, a densely populated neighborhood with almost no grassy area, or severely neglected neighborhoods where schools and other facilities have not been kept up—but even in these cases, warehouses, industrial buildings and even abandoned parking lots can eventually be converted into athletic spaces.

BLOC Ministries, a community development ministry network in Cincinnati whose staff live in the neighborhoods they serve, runs a ministry that combines cost-free professional-level athletic training with wholistic spiritual and academic support. Their TRIBE program works specifically with boys involved in the criminal justice system, offering athletic training, mentoring, and advocacy to those on probation or parole as well as visiting the Hamilton County Youth Center twice a month. The entire operation is run out of what was once an abandoned garage, which has been completely renovated and outfitted as a training and tutoring center, as founding director Jordan Bunch describes:

> It was storage for junk, and it was flooded, and had about two thousand tires in it. It wasn't functionally being used. The location was perfect. It was in our neighborhood within walking distance for most of the kids that we work with, about a block from a school that we work with. It was the perfect amount of space for us to start with, and it had a garage door that could open to the street. The visibility on the street was perfect. We raised money to purchase it, and we received a grant from the attorney general of Ohio to renovate the building. Our ministry has a contractor, and he's got a team of guys who he's teaching to do that work, so they do all of the work on our buildings.

BLOC's willingness to train and employ local people to rejuvenate a local structure led to deep relationship building both with local youth and with public systems, in a way that wouldn't have happened if the facility had been located elsewhere:

> We are two years in and—not much has gone how we originally planned or expected! But it is what it's supposed to be. If you come in on the surface it appears to be a high-level sports training facility, where we are running a few different workouts with kids who come in the afternoon. But for most of the kids that come in, we end up being the ones they come to when they have issues at home, at school, in court. We get to be the ones to pray with them, to have them over for dinner. We are giving the kids, in our opinion, the best training the kids could get no matter where they

go. But we are also bringing the spiritual and relational component that other places may not necessarily bring.

Our relationship with the justice system was a God thing—I got welcomed in by a judge. That's how we see working with the justice system—redirecting boys that are prone to being drawn to the streets before they get too deep in. We've got one kid who I would consider a real success story. He was really deep into the street lifestyle, got arrested, came to us. Now he's on the baseball team at school, pursuing success, and he's lost sixty pounds.

Although community resources are sometimes controlled by people who have an agenda, those who have a good reputation within the community are likely to find ways of being welcomed into the appropriate spaces. Memphis Athletic Ministries, a Christian Community Development ministry in Memphis, Tennessee, serves thousands of children and youth each year at eight locations across the city. Four of these are community centers that were slated to be closed by the city; MAM stepped in and offered to lease the community centers each for $1 per year. The city benefits because their centers are filled with meaningful programming, and MAM gained four facilities in which to serve the children and youth of the city. Two other locations are in churches, where MAM runs full programming--with no formal lease. In one church, MAM contributed $40,000 worth of updates to the church's recreation building before opening programming there. Says MAM Chief Operating Officer Jonathan Torres, "Instead of signing a lease—we try to be the kind of partner no one would ever want to do without." That kind of approach goes a long way.

Sometimes, our choice of location speaks powerfully to the community's sense of ownership and value. Jamie Jessup recalls how the decision to host Camp Clutch in the smallest, most unimpressive rec center in the Winston-Salem system began as a way to keep the camp accessible, but also communicated important biblical truth about the community itself:

> Camp Clutch always sought to connect with the community by engaging them right where they were. When it came to deciding where to house our program, we were fortunate to have several options, ranging from schools to churches, and community facilities. The quality of facilities ranged from relatively modest to state-of-the-art with the latest technology and equipment. We were encouraged by the support we received from many organizations, many of whom were white, upper-middle-class groups, who willingly offered to open their doors to our children, many of whom were Black and under-resourced. However, we believed the idea of taking our children to the beforementioned higher-end facilities would perpetuate the John 1:46 principle expressed by Nathanael and accepted by many people today, within and outside the church, in which they ask, "What good can come out of the hood?"
>
> Being from Nazareth meant coming from an ethnically diverse, low-income community where others perceived you as coming from nothing more than a place where lower-class people, with a lower-class mindset who beget more of the same type of people. Nazareth, like many communities today, was viewed as nothing more than a place of endless poverty, depression, and hopelessness. Many times, the aesthetics of a community evolve into the characteristics we ascribe to the community's inhabitants. For example, examine Nathanael's reaction when he first heard of Jesus, or better yet his place of origin. He said, "Can anything good come from there [Nazareth]?" The devalued perception of the community was such that outsiders devalued the humanity of its people. In terms of valuing a community's conditions, we must refrain from completely absolving the people from their contributions. However, to assume the quality of the city is reflective of the quality of a person while ignoring the systems and structures which contributed to the current state of affairs is dangerous and irresponsible. Those who perpetuate those beliefs: 1) Absolve themselves and the surrounding community from taking action, and 2) Send a message to specific populations that they don't matter, which becomes internalized and perpetuated. Consequently, the result is programming for youth from under-resourced communities housed in "better" spaces outside of where they lived.

Therefore, the message students receive is, "Good things don't come where I'm from, so I must not be good either."

Fully aware of this inconvenient truth, Camp Clutch sought to help change that narrative. The desire led us to choose the Sims Center Recreation Center on the Southside of Winston-Salem. The Southside of Winston is home to one of the highest rates of childhood poverty in America. Although the features at Sims paled in comparison to others, we believed they offered the best option to show the community that greatness is already here and they need not look any further than where they already are. They must understand that Camp Clutch did not introduce the value. We were merely conduits, used by God, to bring attention to that which already existed. We seek to follow the model of Christ who used that which was deemed insignificant and displayed its significance.

Good Neighbors: Remainers, Returners, and Relocators

These stories illustrate a larger point: the right location within the community is key to being effective, but the right relationship to the community is ten times more important. An important concept in Christian Community Development is the simple idea of being a good neighbor—someone who shares life with surrounding people in a healthy way. This idea is rooted in Jesus's teaching that the second great commandment after love the Lord your God with all your heart, with all your soul, with all your mind, and with all your strength, is the simple and profound "golden rule" that we learn as children: love your neighbor as yourself. When pressed about what this command meant, Jesus told the now-familiar story of the good Samaritan, recorded in Luke 10:25-37. When an Israelite man was robbed, beaten, and left for dead along the roadside, a priest and a Levite—supposed to be teachers of God's law, from the man's own culture—walked by without offering help. But a Samaritan, someone on the other side of an ethnic and cultural divide, rescued the man and paid for his healing. It was the Samaritan, Jesus said, who was a "neighbor" to the Israelite man, despite their differences.

A neighbor is someone who makes others' needs as important as his or her own, which is far more important and effective than the quick-fixes and strategic solutions with which many people approach struggling communities. Someone can be the best coach, the best athlete, or the best fundraiser in the world, but if that person does not first love their neighbors, he or she is what 1 Corinthians 13:1 calls "a resounding gong or a clanging cymbal"—in other words, a whole lot of noise and no real impact. Programs run by long-time community members have a higher chance of successful impact, but a sports program can be run entirely by leaders native to the community and still have a reputation for corruption, mistrust, and personal vendettas. A sports program can be run entirely by outsiders—at least for a time—and have a well-deserved reputation as a welcoming and empowering presence. Or, outsiders can come in with a condescending "savior complex," and do more harm than good.

Ultimately, being a neighbor is about being *rooted in the community*, and when neighborhood insiders and those who were once outsiders are able to work together as neighbors, this relational rootedness bolsters the well-being of the whole. Traditionally, Dr. Perkins has taught that those who want to make an impact in a struggling neighborhood should live, work, and worship within that neighborhood if at all possible, and that advice that rings true today. But our lives may follow different patterns; some returners may be able to stay rooted in their original neighborhood while living and working in another part of town, especially in larger cities; some dedicated coaches can make a lifelong impact without ever physically relocating to the neighborhood where most of their athletes live. The important thing is that we are rooted in community together, that we share a common life and purpose. It is never our job to "bring God" to a community; God is already at work in every community. It is our job to find out where and how He is working, join in the work, and let Him draw us together into a common purpose.

Dr. Perkins came to understand the need for cooperation between community leaders of different backgrounds through his own experiences. Although he found success and salvation after he left Mississippi for Los Angeles, the Lord made clear to him that he could not make a real contribution to the town that nurtured him, or to the growing Civil Rights movement of the time, from California. Dr. Perkins relocated back to his native Mendenhall to work with those who had remained there, bringing resources and experiences with him, and eventually inviting others to relocate there to fill certain much-needed roles. In time, Perkins realized that the community could not stand on its own legs without reversing the exodus of the young and the educated from the town, and focused energy on helping successful young people return like himself to make a home. Dr. Perkins ultimately framed his ideas about community presence in terms of three types of "relocators:" remainers, returners, and relocators, all working together for the community's good. The Sports world is full of all three types.

Remainers

Remainers have never left the community, but "relocate" socially into roles of leadership and influence. Remainers make up the lifeblood of any community, and are the core of the world of community sports. From the volunteer parents, to the coaches who sustain the local Pop Warner league, to the faithful fan base at the high school or college football game, to the church deacon who chaplains the basketball team at the high school where he once played point guard, the "remainers" hold their community together. Empowering "remainers" to build and shepherd the community is an essential part of Christian Community Development. For remainers, being a good neighbor increasingly means being a wise leader, offering experience and wisdom that few others have, and shepherding the young as they navigate difficult environments, where leadership has often been co-opted by outside forces or absent altogether. These leaders are found in the most unlikely places. It's the grandmother running concessions at the high school football game, who has played piano at the church around the corner for forty years; it's the man who works early mornings as a janitor, has been coaching little league without pay for a decade, and is the first person to seek out the middle schooler who missed school the last four days; it's the mother who always has two or three of her daughter's friends riding home with her after practice. These people are the backbone of the community, embodying and living out a wisdom and grace that no school could teach. They are often overlooked, and sometimes even hard to find; a good first step is to ask the young people who they trust and turn to. These are the people who, if simply given access to the right resources, already know how to make the community thrive. Philadelphia's Buddy Martinez is an excellent example:

> You cannot talk about Timoteo without talking about Buddy, born and raised in Philly. Several years ago, one of the youth from the youth group I (Chris) was working with asked if our church could put a team in Timoteo flag football. Buddy, fresh outta high school, was the first person I asked to assist me on this new venture. One thing we had in common was a passion for football.

I'll never forget that first year we would call each other daily and our conversations would last for hours talking about strategies and how we could improve the team. We didn't do too bad the first year, but in our second year I noticed a slight change with Buddy when it came to talking about the team. I noticed that we not only talked strategy, but we started talking about the players themselves, and I even noticed Buddy calling them "my kids." It didn't take long for people to see that Buddy was gifted working with youth, and Timoteo provided the opportunity for him to do just that. By year three, I stepped aside and allowed Buddy to run the team as the head coach. As a remainer Buddy was able to connect with the youth in a different manner than I was able to, and it was amazing to see Buddy's leadership grow.

It didn't take long before Buddy started delegating "power" to other up-and-coming leaders who wanted to help run the team. Buddy was able to see the potential in others and he set the table for them to serve and discover their own gifts. Buddy was the glue that has brought together many multiplex relationships in Timoteo. Buddy realized that our success can become our ruin, as no one person can do it all, and that a collection of people are needed to accomplish great work. Initially Buddy would sit with youth and help the fill out their FAFSA or an application for their first job. Though this still happens from time to time, Buddy realized the importance of partnering with other organizations already doing this stuff effectively and on a larger scale.

When asked what motivated him in his work with Timoteo, he said without hesitation, "I love creating moments." He went on to elaborate, "I love those moments that change a kid's life, the moment they catch their first pass, when they make it into a highlight or top ten and they are able to show their parents or classmates. I love the moments when they get their first job with Timoteo and they show pride in their work. I love the moment when they realize they are a part of something greater than themselves, they are a part of a family." Jesus said if you want to find your life, you will lose it (Mt 16:25). Buddy is the manifestation of this passage, as he has given of himself to his community and the community is in a better place because of it.

If you are a *remainer*, someone who has poured your heart and soul into your hometown for years, who has stayed dedicated through the good times and the bad, who has seen people come and go and knows who is there for the long haul, who knows the local sports world from the quarterbacks to the water boys, this book is the perfect tool for you. In the pages to come we will explore ways to empower the legacy that years of faithfulness and dedication can have in the community you have loved, and has loved you back, since you were young.

Relocators

Relocators in the literal sense are people who (like Coach Wayne Gordon) have moved into a struggling community with the hope of making a contribution toward a brighter future for the people who live there. At the professional and college levels, coaches move around often, and are faced with the challenge of understanding and living alongside a new set of neighbors with a new set of blessings and challenges. In some denominations, pastors will serve many different communities across their lifetimes; parachurch youth workers and other outreach ministers sometimes relocate to a new community out of a sense of calling. Parents who move to a new city for work or other reasons seek out sports activities for their children, and volunteer as coaches, boosters, or team parents as a way to get to know their neighbors and become active in community life.

For relocators, the process of becoming a good neighbor is especially important, even more so if the relocator is arriving in an already privileged position—whether that privilege be social, financial, educational, or the kind of privilege of position that pastors and coaches have. It is important for relocators to respect and listen to the community, rather than assuming that they have brought the solutions with them, and that doing things "their way" will always work. This can be a very challenging, but very rewarding process.

Jeff Thompson reflects on the process of relocating to West Baltimore after growing up in Virginia, playing college football, and starting a career in nonprofit work:

> For me, in a sports context, taking root in the community has taken on the form of gathering wisdom, inquiring about the neighborhood, constantly, from indigenous community members and youth workers (especially those involved in sports) regarding the climate of the neighborhood and it's youth. It has also meant inquiring, honoring and seeking to support the efforts of those already present, doing (or attempting to do) the work of reaching youth in the community (especially through sports). The more sports-based youth workers have felt that we've supported and honored them and their efforts, the more they have joyfully chosen to do everything in their power to aid our program in reaching the youth in the neighborhood. From freely allowing us to use their recreational facilities to showing up weekly to support us, we've seen these leaders become refreshed and hopeful through our efforts, simply because they feel more supported, listened to, and a part of a collective effort to reach the community."

Chris Lahr grew up in northern Indiana, attended college at Eastern University outside of Philadelphia, and relocated to Kensington in North Philadelphia after seminary, where he soon began working with Timoteo Sports:

> The most important thing for a relocator is to get connected to the community, and this only happens with time. The more of an outsider you are to the community, the more important it is for you to spend a great deal of time in the community you serve. Too often outsiders are quick to want to use their "gifts" in the church or a particular ministry, but the greater the cultural gap, the longer this process should be—I have learned it is important to earn the right to use your gifts! The first step in relocation is simply "being." It is more important to get to know people than to "fix" them, or even to correct the great injustices that surround you in your new life.
>
> In 2000 my family moved to North Philadelphia with the desire to learn the meaning of community and how to be a neighbor. I will never forget meeting our next-door neighbors the first year. Connected to us on one side was an elderly couple that listened to their music very loudly because they were going deaf. On the other side was a much younger couple that listened to their music loudly

because, well, they liked listening to their music loudly. The young lady living next to us (I will call her Maria) didn't go out much when we first moved in. It took several months before she built enough trust even to talk to us. I'll never forget about a year into our being in Philly I was sitting on our porch watching the world go by as Maria talked with another neighborhood lady. When their conversation was done, Maria looked at me and said, "Can you believe that? I just talked to a neighbor!" I didn't know what to say—I wished I had a trophy or something to give her for her achievement! She then went on to say, "You don't understand, I've lived here for over ten years and I'm the neighborhood bitch, I don't talk to anybody. But I see the way you and Lara interact with the neighbors and I wanted to give it a try, and I like it! Besides, the way I see your marriage, it gives me hope that marriage actually works!"

After two years we ended up moving from that block to a house a couple miles away. We went several years without seeing Maria. Then just last year we went by her house as we were getting ready to take a vanload of food to our church neighborhood. When we saw Maria on the porch we pulled the van over and started talking. We asked if she wanted some of the food we had, and she not only said yes, but she asked if there was enough for her neighbors! She then started going door to door asking the neighbors if they wanted to come out and get some food. She had transformed from "neighborhood bitch" to neighborhood mama! She informed us that she was getting ready to move out of state, but then gave us her number and said if we are ever back in the neighborhood with food, give her a call and she would call all of the neighbors for us to come out! Following Jesus and being a good neighbor is not "sexy." It is about living your life well, no matter what context you find yourself in. As we do this, transformation happens—not only in others, but in ourselves as well.

John Perkins once said that it takes about ten years for a relocator to start seeing the fruit of their work in the community. The goal of relocation is never assimilation. Just because you wear a hoodie, eat cheesesteaks and like the Eagles doesn't mean you have "arrived" in Philadelphia. The real goal is to stay humble and to allow others from the community to flourish and rise to leadership in their own community, while you learn from them and use your gifts to do the work God has for you there:

> "Go to the people,
> Live among them.

Learn from them.
Start with what they know.
Build on what they have:
But of the best leaders,
When their work is done,
The people all remark
'We have done it ourselves.'"
– Old Chinese Poem

If you are a *relocator*, once an outsider, now seeking to make a redemptive difference in a new community, this book is the perfect tool for you. In the chapters to come, we will explore how to listen to and learn about the community, to seek out where God is already moving and to get involved, to make your own contribution and help organize and empower the contributions of others, and how to advocate for your neighbors in a way that brings about justice and peace—using the sports that you love as a tool to create the community that gives you and your neighbors hope for the future.

Returners

Returners are people who, like Dr. Perkins, grew up in a struggling community, left to pursue education, employment, or other opportunities, and ultimately returned home out of a desire to make a difference to the family and community that nurtured them. North America is a very mobile society, and for decades, communities with fewer resources have watched young people with education and leadership skills leave for other places with more opportunities; it is hard for our neighborhoods to experience a turnaround until some of those young people decide to stay or return and make a home in the place they were raised. The sports world is filled with returners, and especially with those who hope to be returners—we often hear our young athletes express cherished dreams of what they want to do when they "come home" after their athletic career is done and what sort of job they want to have after college: "When I get back, I'm gonna fix up that old house on the corner – my kids are gonna run all around in that big backyard!" "When I get back, every single kid on this playground is gonna have a new coat and new shoes – I'll make sure of it!" "When I get back, I'm gonna tell kids like me how I made it – so they can do it too!"

Our young people are nurturing dreams of succeeding for themselves and making things better for the people they love. A key part of effective community development is making these dreams possible by creating an environment where those who have left for education or career advancement can return, thrive, and raise families. Returners who have experienced the blessings and challenges of the community as children and youth, and who have also gained experience, education, skills and perspectives in other places, are in a unique position to help imagine and contribute to solutions for the community's future. For returners, the desire to be a good neighbor has almost certainly been part of the decision to return. Still, for returners to be effective, they need to avoid the pitfalls of pride in the same way relocators do, and immerse themselves in lifting others up.

In Charleston, West Virginia, Joshua "Cookie" Miller tells the story of how he grew up on the city's West Side, and how his love for basketball and his desire to serve his community led him from being temporarily homeless, to a Division One basketball program, to living in Poland, to coaching at an HBCU, and finally to founding the community-based Second Avenue League. His story is a striking example of a "returner" whose love for sports allowed him to gather experiences across the globe and across the social spectrum, and whose love for his family and community led him to ultimately re-root himself in the neighborhood that raised him. His story is emblematic of the dreams of many young athletes, and begins in a struggling neighborhood, with a personal struggle to overcome:

> I grew up surrounded by family. I was one of the few of my friends who lived with both my parents. I have four older sisters, and by high school I had fifteen nieces and nephews—I have twenty-two now. A lot of families met up once a week for a meal after church, but my house was a meetup spot for our whole extended family every night after work.
>
> My dad had worked at the power company for nineteen years, until he went in with his brother on a business venture of turning a church building into a daycare. It didn't pan out, and my mom's income was not enough to keep our house. It was a difficult and stressful time. We moved around the city for a while, and we were homeless for a year and half. It made me a shy, observant person—I didn't say too much during those years, and I didn't understand how it was that I had this huge family, but we were sometimes living in a hotel. Finally, we settled in a house on Second Avenue, on the West Side of Charleston.
>
> There was always a lot of action on the West Side. People stood on the street corners looking for drugs—cell phones were just coming out, so most people would watch for a car to pull up, and they would argue over who would get to buy the drugs. If the drugs were bad or the sale went wrong, there would be violence. When we were young we didn't know what it was all about, but as we got older we came to understand what was going on right in front of our faces. If everyone wasn't at my house they would be at my grandmother's house in Washington Manor, a housing project

behind downtown, a thirty-minute walk away. That neighborhood was about the same as mine—prostitutes, stabbings, police brutality, robberies. I saw all of that growing up.

For Joshua, sports were both an escape, and a healing experience that built community and confidence:

The Martin Luther King Jr. Community Center near Washington Manor was really an outlet for us. Near my house there was an outdoor court and an old school that had been transformed into a community center called the Second Avenue Center—eventually, when the city was closing down buildings, a nearby church bought the community center from the city for a dollar. A lot of my friends and I would play basketball or football there, and ride our bikes around the neighborhood together.

Football was my first love, my number one sport. I started playing when I was six. I could use up a lot of anger just making contact on the field. My speed came from running from dogs in the 'hood—or running from trouble when something was going on (when someone started running, you ran too—there wasn't any asking questions). I started playing basketball at seven or eight, but I'm 5'7", so at first basketball looked out of reach. But I eventually decided I didn't want to get hit all the time on the football field. As I spent more time on basketball, the game became slower to me, and I started to be able to see plays on the court before they even happened.

As Joshua realized that his athletic talent could take him places, he also realized over time how much community support would play into balancing his competing commitments:

My ninth and tenth grade years were good years for me academically. But in my eleventh and twelfth grade years, I didn't want to be on the West Side anymore, and I wanted to get out of my living situation. I had a girlfriend in St. Albans (a suburb) who lived in a great neighborhood. Right after school I'd go straight to St. Albans on the bus. I got behind in school, so I didn't finish strong. I was lucky to have great parents, and my dad had been talking to a coach at Gulf Shore Academy in Florida who had sent several players to Division One colleges. We were on our way to Florida, and a good friend of my dad's named Richard Hoffmaster, from Martinsburg (a West Virginia suburb near DC) called and told my dad that there was a new prep school opening up in Cincinnati, and he'd told the coach I'd be coming down. The coach said, "If you're saying he can play, he has a position on the team—tell him to bring his things with him!"

Attending Harmony Prep, I reunited with an old friend from Huntington, O.J. Mayo (the #1 high school player in the nation at the time) and Bill (Henry) Walker (#2 or #3 after Derrick Rose, I can't remember), on the AAU Circuit with the D1 Greyhounds. I played against Derrick, James Harden, Brandon Jennings, DeAndre Jordan, Eric Gordon, Kevin Love, Tyrek Evans, a number of people who really made it. Isaiah Thomas was on my all-star team at a camp. Out of thirty people at that camp, almost twenty eventually played in the NBA. I had hardly ever seen anyone make it to the next level, but when I saw all the top Division One coaches lined up to see us with a paper in their hands, and my name was on that paper, I realized: this could happen. I held my own, and after that my dorm room and my house were full of letters from colleges.

I had a number of Division One offers. I chose Nebraska, a Big 12 school; my girlfriend was pregnant with our daughter, and Nebraska would let me live off-campus with her. Looking back on it, we were young and seventeen hours from home, doing it on our own with our first child, and we didn't know how much help we would need. Halfway through my first year, she became pregnant with our second daughter. My freshman and sophomore years were focused on them. I held my own on the court, and most people saw me as successful—I'm still 2nd all-time as a freshman and sophomore in steals, assists, and turnover ratio at Nebraska, behind Tyrone Lue—but I didn't have enough time to work on my craft to get to the level that I wanted to get to. I realized that we needed to be closer to home.

Transferring to another Division One school would mean sitting out a year, so instead I transferred to West Virginia State, a Division Two Historically Black University where one of my friends was playing, located between Charleston and St. Albans. Coming home was one of the best decisions of my life. I could see who was really there for me, who really cared about me. I was able to be hands-on with my community, instead of them just watching me on TV. I went to schools to talk, and told people what West Virginia State University was all about.

With help from his family, a coach, a professor, and a host of others, basketball took Joshua across the world—and right back into the heart of his community:

My junior year, I took a class where I had to create a portfolio for myself as an event director. I chose starting a basketball league and as I got more detailed it hit me that I could start a summer league in my own community, at the Second Avenue Center that the church had bought. I took the idea to the pastor, who was a strong influence in my life, and he said he would help. We weren't sure about the referees and the jerseys. The first summer of the Second Avenue League, we used borrowed jerseys from the college, and he and I were the referees. The number one thing I was hoping for was to have a consistent, positive thing going on in the neighborhood for all ages. That first summer we had eight teams. It was a struggle—the court was bad, the rims were bent and the loops were messed up so we had to zip tie the nets up. The second year, someone donated new rims. The fourth year, we were able to incorporate more of the youth from the neighborhood in the process, and it really took off.

A week after college ended, my coach hooked me up with an agent out of Las Vegas who held a showcase camp every year, with some NBA coaches and scouts there, and a lot of overseas general managers and coaches in the room. The owners of a Polish team called the Siarka Tarnobrzek made me the best offer, so for the next five years, I spent eight months out of the year in Poland, and four months in West Virginia, back with my family and running the Second Avenue League.

I never learned much Polish—plenty of people spoke English. Most Polish people only saw Black people on television, and I had a lot of hair then; people were pretty "hands on" seeing a real black person for the first time! The people there were very supportive. I guess I'm too friendly sometimes, and soon I was throwing shoes and shirts and other souvenirs out the window to the Polish kids, and they were knocking on the door every hour of the day, throwing things at my window to get my attention—by the time I left I didn't take a single thing back with me besides my trophies. The team told me I had to move to a new apartment complex, and try to be a little less friendly!

(photo by Natasha Hairston-Tyson)

I had full custody of my daughters since 2012, and when I was overseas my mother and father took care of them. After five years of spending over half the year in Poland playing basketball my mother got sick, and I came home. It was a hard time, giving up something that I had been doing the majority of my life over something beyond my control.

I hadn't graduated from college, and I set up a meeting with my coach about finishing my degree and maybe eventually running camps or tournaments in the college's new gym. Two weeks later he called and told me that the head assistant job had opened up, and the first person who came to his mind was me. I asked him to give me a couple days to talk it over with my family. Within two days I told him I was coming home. This is my third year coaching college basketball, I've walked across the stage with my bachelor's degree, and I still run the Second Avenue League in the summers.

I've learned that failure is not an option. What I didn't have, I wanted to bring that to my community. Basketball was my outlet to get out of Charleston—and then to bring a summer league to the community that can be other people's way of chasing their dreams and aspirations.

Joshua's story is an example of a returning leader who used his athletic talent, community support, and personal drive first as tools to navigate difficult circumstances, then as a launching pad for personal success, and then as a means to serve and empower the community that raised him. Stories like these, stories that show us the many ways that sports can contribute to personal and community wholeness, are the core of why sports are such an excellent tool for community development.

If you are a *returner*, or you hope to be, if you want to make your permanent home in the place where you were raised but are not sure if you can, this book is the perfect tool for you. In the following pages we will explore the balance between deepening roots and broadening horizons, and sift through strategies for making the dream of so many young athletes—using a passion for sports to build a better life for those they love—an impactful reality.

Whether we arrived yesterday or were born at the county hospital, good community leadership takes skill, faith, humility, and dedication. The Bible teaches us that no matter who we are, we need each other. Just like the many different positions on a well-rounded sports team, we all have something to offer one another, and we cannot win until we learn to work together. Successful community development is a collaboration between those who have spent their lives in the community, those who have relocated there to contribute to the community's well-being, and those who have returned to reinvest even after having the opportunity to leave. The sports world is filled with all of these, and whichever of these you may be, the most important starting point is to be a good neighbor.

This brings us to our next idea—to be good neighbors, let alone good leaders, we first need to be good listeners.

Listening: Wisdom & Culture

It was about a year after the Lahr family moved to Philadelphia that we started actively getting involved in our local church, beyond simple attendance. During that first year we took time to get to know people, to eat good Hispanic food (it was a predominantly Puerto Rican church), and to listen. About a year in, one of the church leaders asked me (Chris) if I would be interested in helping out with the youth group. Up to this point they had a few girls attending their weekly meeting, and they wanted to figure out how to reach out to the guys in the neighborhood. We listened to a couple youth, who stated they were interested in playing basketball in the church's run-down gym. It wasn't your typical youth group meeting of playing a few games and then going through a Bible study, but once we started playing basketball it didn't take long for the word to hit the streets.

Soon we had a few guys who were connected to the church, in their upper teens and lower twenties, coming out to ball on a weekly basis. We would throw open the side door and sit on the steps to cool off between games, which gave us a chance to connect with several neighbors. Within a few months the gym was filled with youth from the community playing ball—after six months we had about 40 guys coming to our church to play, and it became a safe place where positive relationships were being built. We realized we were quickly growing out of the gym, so we decided to gather all of the people over the age of 18, and we had a talk. We informed them that this was supposed to be a "youth ministry" and that if they want to continue to stay they would need to be "youth workers." Every one of them agreed! We began training them on how to effectively mentor and minister to these youth. Because the crowd had become so big, this new group of youth workers used their intellect and creativity to create new programming and ways to connect with the youth, and built relationships to the point that we could introduce weekly Bible studies that actively involved the youth (Bible study is very important, but it is more effective if a relationship is built). Listening to the community is important, will sometimes cause us to think and act outside of traditional ministry models.

To be good leaders, we first have to be good neighbors. And to be good neighbors, we need to learn to be good listeners, learning about the people and places that surround us. We become rooted by *listening to the community.*

Christian Community Development is grounded in the idea that the best solutions to a community's problems will come from within the community itself. Who better to create a path forward than the people who know the strengths and struggles of their friends and neighbors, who have experienced the pains and joys that come from daily life in the neighborhood? Anyone—whether a native or a relocator—who wants to help develop the community's future, needs to listen to the collective wisdom of the people. The value of listening is ultimately grounded in the Bible's teaching that we are all equally made in the image of God (Genesis 1:27), and that we all have something to contribute towards a collective wholeness (Ephesians 4:16). Too often, in our poorest communities, negative stereotypes and systems of disadvantage have led to the image of God reflected in the people and their contributions being neglected and ignored. Some of these people have even accepted the belief they have little or nothing to offer. In our sports programs, we have all encountered young people who have little idea of their potential, or who have been denied opportunities to use it. Listening to the community helps us to overcome this by respecting and empowering the image of God in our neighbors.

Listening to the community is an important way to avoid *paternalism.* Paternalism is the idea that outsiders with expertise need to "fix" the community and the people in it. Paternalism is sometimes obvious, when arrogant and intrusive "helpers" try to impose unhelpful solutions without consulting the people involved. But paternalism can sneak up on us—subtle attitudes about education or money or culture can end up excluding the ideas of the people who could help the most. Listening to the community is one of the most important ways to make sure the community's wisdom, knowledge, skills and input are valued, employed, and empowered.

Asset-Based Thinking

People commonly talk about distressed communities in terms of problems that need to be solved, quoting statistics about crime, dropout rates, low incomes, or other markers of poor social health. While points of community pain are important to understand, more constructive solutions present themselves when we move from a *deficit-based approach* to an *asset-based approach.* Deficit-based thinking identifies needs within the community, but often leads to solutions that primarily involve outside experts and people with resources meeting those needs. This approach can stave off problems temporarily, but often fails to address the root causes, and can lead to long-term dependency on outside resources. *Asset-Based Community Development*, first developed at Northwestern University in the 1990s, moves from identifying problems to surveying the assets available in a neighborhood to create sustainable solutions from inside the community. Assets include institutional assets (such as libraries, parks, and schools), private assets (such as buildings and businesses), and most importantly, the skills, talents, and potential of the people that make up the community itself.

One asset you will almost always find in a community? Sports. For those in sports ministry, asset-based thinking means asking: what can we do with what we have? Every community has parks, schools, buildings, and probably rec centers, adults who played sports when they were younger, and usually existing community sports leagues. These are the starting points for moving forward.

This kind of thinking is just as important in our spiritual reflections and discipleship. Oftentimes, ministries to distressed communities use language that implies that they are "bringing Jesus" to the community. But when we take up this kind of work, it is important to remember that the Bible tells us that *God is already there*. Not only is God everywhere at all times (Jeremiah 23:23-24, Psalm 15:3), He is present in the lives, prayers, and work of the Christians already living in the community (Matthew 18:20). Christians have been laboring faithfully for years in nearly every distressed community in North America. Doing ministry among the poor is not about heroically bringing in the answers everyone has been waiting for—it is about joining in with the work God is already doing through the people he has called there. To do this requires us to carefully listen to and understand those who have faithfully endured the community's struggles and triumphs for years.

Listening to the community is about harnessing the passions, talents, and assets of the people there to meet the needs of the people there. Ultimately, we want to do what works for the community—not repackage what worked somewhere else, or project the preferences of a few leaders onto everyone else. What works in Atlanta won't necessarily work in Alaska, and just because the executive director likes baseball doesn't mean everyone else will. We want to see the gifts and energy of our neighbors awakened and channeled in a way that breathes life and power into to community as a whole. And when it comes to harnessing passions, developing talents, and mobilizing energy, sports are an excellent place to start.

Listening to the Community and Sports Ministry

For those who start and run programs, a first important question is: are sports even needed? We love sports, and so we are eager to share what we love, but does the community perceive the need? And while most communities are receptive to a ministry-focused youth sports program, do community-run programs already exist? Sometimes, adding energy and resources to a community-run program may be far more effective than starting a new one. And which sports does the community perceive a need for? Which sports are already popular with the community? It is likely that parents and other volunteers could coach, referee, and organize these sports easily. Is there a perceived willingness to learn and support new sports? In any of these cases, buy-in from the community is key.

Chris Lahr reflects on experiences with different sports in Philadelphia:

> "When considering starting a sports program, it is important to listen to the community to discover what people there are passionate about. We had a multi-million-dollar facility built in one of our neighborhoods, but it is grossly underutilized because the main sport they push is squash. What it "squash," you ask? Exactly—and no one in the neighborhood knows what it is either. Just because squash or soccer works in your community doesn't necessarily mean it will work in another. At the same time, I'm convinced that if you show passion for something and show a real interest in youth you can get them to do just about anything, and have found that as we have connected with the youth in the neighborhood through sports that they know, we have been able to introduce different sports and other ideas. It's all about listening and staying relationally rooted.
>
> Another thing—don't shy away from new sports introduced to you from the community that you are not familiar with. I remember a young person teaching me how to play chess (sport? not a sport? up for debate) one year. He wasn't the greatest of teachers, as each game he would destroy me and I was left figuring that there had to be more to this game, a strategy that I needed to figure out. So I did the unthinkable: I studied chess. I read books about chess, I watched videos and even went to a chess tournament to observe. It wasn't long before I was schooling the young man, and a love for chess began to grow among many youth in Kensington (one of the poorest neighborhoods in Philly). People asked if I was "nerdifying the hood," but I assured them that it was the youth nerdifying me. Eventually we started a very successful chess club for a few years, and several members that even competed in local chess tournaments. Whatever you find yourself doing, do it with passion and excellence. If you connect to where people are and allow their passions to become your passions, God can use it to bring about a very successful ministry.

There are some aspects of listening to the community—and some pitfalls—that relate specifically to youth sports. One issue that continues to evolve in youth sports is the hyper-involvement of certain parents in their child's athletic life. A leader eager to "listen to the community" about the best way to use athletics for community development ministry is likely to immediately hear certain strong voices urging him or her to play certain athletes or not to hire certain coaches, or even parents who simply want to talk at length—in a manner that may be anything from endearingly supportive to loudly accusatory—about their own child's capabilities, potential, and supposed needs. When we listen to the community, we need to make sure we are listening to *representative* voices. We need to make sure that we are listening to the community as a whole, and seeking the good of the community as a whole, rather than being sidetracked by special or personal interests. One of the best ways to do this is to seek out diverse and representative members of the community for input.

At the same time, for coaches of youth teams, especially older youth, listening to players can be more important than some realize. Although popular movies and memories of "the good old days" often glorify tough, no-nonsense coaches who whip listless boys into shape, the reality of using athletics as a community development tool has a lot more to do with bringing out and forming the leadership of young people who have grown up too fast than it does with imposing abstract forms of discipline on those who need to grow up.

Timoteo's Eric Moore has found that the best listening sometimes happens in the downtimes.

> To have an effective mentoring program you need mentors who know how to listen. A sports program isn't effective if the final goal is winning championships. An effective coach is concerned with bringing about transformation through player development and mentoring. One such coach is Eric Moore of Timoteo Sports. Eric was a New York cop living in Philadelphia when he came across Timoteo. Eric has a servant's heart, and when asked by his pastor to take over the church's flag football team he jumped at the opportunity.

Eric has demonstrated the importance of listening to his players. Eric has a passion to coach, but he realizes that we must also coach kids in their school decisions and their life decisions. Eric would say it is through the rigors of a football practice that you build a bond with the youth and you begin a relationship with them. He would also say that the field is only the beginning of a real mentoring relationship.

One of the things that Eric has taught me (Chris) is the importance of the car ride. Every week as practice concludes, players need a ride home to places scattered throughout the city. It is not uncommon for these rides to take at least an hour more of your time. For many coaches this may seem to be a nuisance after a long day. Eric taught me that this can be one of the most important moments in coaching a kid – the ride home. Eric is a great listener, and it is often in the context of these car rides home that he would learn about the kids' families, their school situation, and of course their love life (or lack thereof)! Coach Eric listens, and he coaches at a deeper level than most. For effective mentoring and community development to occur, it is important that we listen well to our youth, to discover their real needs, and be moved with compassion to do something about those needs.

Eric is also very helpful on a staff level, as he is also an active listener there as well. Every organization needs an Eric to bounce things off of and to receive constructive criticism and words of wisdom to help the organization move forward. Eric is also a great encourager. It's easy to redirect your players when they mess up on the field, but it is also important to build them up when they do something right. Active listening leads to meaningful encouragement and the ability to see a future leader when others only see a troubled youth.

The *Leadership Scale for Sports* is a research tool used for decades by sports psychologists to measure aspects of sport leadership such as democratic vs. autocratic coaching behaviors, social support for athletes, training and instruction, and positive motivational feedback. Sport Psychology researchers Daniel Gould and Robert Weinberg note that significant differences can be found both across nationalities, and across sports within a single culture, as to which styles of motivation, support, and decision-making produce the best results, and note in particular that autocratic coaching is *negatively* associated with the kind of empowering leadership development of the young on which Christian Community Development depends (in particular, with what psychologists call "internal locus of control," a belief that one can influence one's own destiny and future) (Weinberg & Gould, 2007, 217-219). Those of us who want to use sports to develop the capacities of our community need to listen carefully to understand both community norms and the development and motivation of individual athletes, and choose a leadership and coaching style that will bring out the best in the people we are investing in. The approach will vary by sport—while the culture of basketball continues to trend toward player involvement in decision-making, for instance, football by nature remains more dependent on executing pre-structured plays. In any case, listening to your players does *not* mean the team becomes a full-on democracy where the coach merely executes the will of the athletes. Structure, execution, and authority are important—and at the same time, so is meeting the needs and empowering the talents of the athletes and others involved. To do this well requires a skill set that is of great importance for those whom God has called to develop our distressed communities: *cultural competence.*

Listening and Cultural Competence

Dr. Soong-Chan Rah (2010), professor at North Park Theological Seminary, writes in his book *Many Colors: Cultural Intelligence for a Changing Church* that "one definition [of culture] is a 'shared (collective within society), socially learned knowledge, and patterns of behavior.' Culture is 'acquired knowledge, lived experience, that helps you navigate the society you live in and provides guidelines for your interaction with others.' Culture, therefore, operates on the individual as well as the societal level" (23).

Culture is the shared knowledge that governs what we consider to be appropriate behavior and interaction. Whole cities and regions can have a culture of their own: businesses in Boston tend to close much earlier than in New York, not because of any law, but simply because of local behavior patterns. Neighborhoods can have cultures of their own: do people ride bikes on the sidewalk? How late is too late to play piano or drums in your house? The answers will probably be different in Flatbush and Farmington Hills. Families and larger people groups have cultures: in some families, it may be fine to shout from the kitchen to the living room: "Grandma, where did you put my shoes?" but in a family from another cultural background, it might be considered disrespectful to speak to an elderly family member with a loud voice and no eye contact. Unwritten cultural norms influence our decisions and behavior about everything from how we put the garbage on the curb to how we find a spouse.

Even sports teams and leagues develop cultures of their own. If a player has a suggestion for the coach, do they say it out loud in a huddle, make an appointment to talk about it later, or say nothing at all? How late for practice is "too late?" Are certain respected players allowed to correct and instruct the others? Are practices open to parents and friends, or closed? Hockey teams and basketball teams tend to react very differently when a fight breaks out mid-game. If an athlete can't pay the league fee, is it formally waived? Does someone step up and pay it for him? Or does the athlete ask someone in his community to pay his way, and the league never finds out?

Listening to the community means learning the community's culture—or cultures. Some communities are very culturally diverse, while others are made up mainly of families from a single ethnic background who have lived there for decades. For those who do sports ministry in distressed communities, it is important for the ministry to *blend well with the culture of the community*, and it is important for the ministry itself to develop a healthy *organizational culture* of its own.

When the coaches and ministry leaders have different cultural backgrounds from the communities they serve, it can be easy for unexpected conflict to emerge. For instance, what is an appropriate reason to miss practice? Nearly all North American cultures agree that missing practice for a doctor's appointment is fine, but we have seen sharp cultural disagreements over whether an athlete has done the right thing if he is late to practice because his grandmother came home with a load of groceries, and he stayed back to help her. Some cultures place responsibility for timeliness with the family as a whole, while other cultures might prioritize helping an elderly family member over the time constraints of a league that only one family member belongs to. It is even possible that a coach being stern with an athlete over being late for this reason, while his family expects helping the elderly to take precedent, could put the athlete in such an uncomfortable position that he quits the team entirely rather than choose between disappointing two adults whom he respects (his coach and his grandmother). At play here are deep cultural issues—time dynamics, extended family, individual responsibility, and the "pecking order" of community leaders.

Sometimes, the issue can seem frustratingly simple, but still stem from deeper cultural differences. In a neighborhood where few people have cars and some don't have cell phone service, who is responsible for rides to practice, and how are they arranged? Do coaches do most of the pickups? Do a few parents arrange the rides? Do the athletes ask for rides themselves, and how far in advance? Do most of the athletes have personal control over their whereabouts—and so coaches should instruct them to be home at the time of pickup—or do family members or others in authority sometimes insist the athlete be somewhere else on short notice?

In Baltimore, Jeff Thompson notices that many coaches have a steep learning curve understanding the reality of their athletes when they are looking for a way to get to practice:

> We see a common frustration in our relocating and some returning youth workers in the beginning of their time of service: before long, they begin griping, "This teenager lives seven blocks away, literally a fifteen minute walk, why does he need me to pick him up?"
>
> In the mind of someone not as familiar with local culture dynamics, this seems like a form of laziness or lack of initiative. The teen, on the other hand, is very familiar with the realities of what has been termed "hood hopping." Seven blocks to the field means crossing three different neighborhoods, which function like territories. Walking by themselves conveys vulnerability and makes them an easy "target," while walking with a group of peers portrays a sense of tension, rivalry and even disrespect, signaling that they feel comfortable enough to bring their own crew past the neighborhood like they "own" it. With these dynamics at play, weekly commutes on foot don't work out in the favor of the teen—there may be no safe way to regularly walk these seven blocks at all. This is a major hindrance to him participating in something like a sports team, unless someone uses their resources (their time, their car, their willingness to understand) to support him.

An important cultural reality like this one shapes a young person's choices and prospects but can be nearly impossible for someone who hasn't lived through the neighborhood's realities to understand, unless that person is willing to listen carefully for cultural understanding. Someone who wants to help but doesn't listen carefully may project damaging labels onto the teen such as "lazy" or "entitled." But someone who is willing to listen with understanding in mind can gain insight into the neighborhood's challenges and make a big difference in what that teen has access to.

Because culture affects nearly every aspect of our lives, issues with cultural dynamics will emerge in the most surprising places. There is no "right way" to solve these challenges that we can present in this book—these issues can only be resolved through careful, prayerful listening, and a Christ-like attitude that puts the needs of others ahead of oneself, and makes the needs of the most vulnerable as a priority in the community.

However, it is possible to develop what is called *cultural competence*, or knowledge and skills that help navigate relationship-building across cultures. Cultural competence has been central to global missions and North American community development for a long time, and as North America and the North American church diversify, these skills are becoming increasingly essential for ministry of all kinds. We encourage those who coach and mentor in our distressed communities to learn from the growing number of resources that exist to train ministers, educators, and youth workers in cultural competence. The following paragraphs outline some essential cross-cultural concepts that come up commonly in sports ministry.

DOMINANT-CULTURE LEADERS: Nearly all regions have a dominant culture (which may or may not be the majority), and other subcultures. In many sports programs, as well as in community development, a disproportionate number of leaders come from the dominant North American culture, which emphasizes college-educated leadership and certain Northern European values like individualism and independence. Culture to a person is like water to a fish: one tends not to notice it when one is surrounded by it. This is especially true for people who closely align with a region's dominant culture, and haven't often had to think about what it would be like for their habits and seemingly "common-sense" decisions not to be immediately understood by those around them. People from the dominant culture who occupy positions of leadership—including coaches, athletic directors, educators, youth workers, and ministers—need to make a special effort to understand how their cultural orientation may be different from those they are working with, and the impact that might have, and learn how to make room for and collaborate with leaders of other cultural orientations.

COLLECTIVE VS. INDIVIDUAL RESPONSIBILITY: Global cultures vary highly regarding individual and collective responsibility. For instance, when someone has an emergency medical expense, do they borrow the money and slowly pay it off (individualist), or is their family or community responsible for finding a way to pay the bill (collectivist)? The dominant North American culture is one of the most individualistic in the world, while many North American subcultures are more collectivist. Team dynamics are incredibly important to most sports, and the individualistic or collectivist orientation of the athletes can make an important difference in how team dynamics work. Will singling out an athlete for public reprimand motivate her to work harder? Will it cause other athletes to put pressure on her to perform? Or will it cause other athletes to lose respect for her? Or to deflect responsibility onto themselves to save her public embarrassment? The answers to these questions can depend highly on the individualistic or collectivist cultural orientation of the athletes involved. Individualist cultures are far more likely to emphasize personal responsibility and personal rewards, while collectivist cultures develop complex behavior patterns that determine how responsibility will be shared. Understanding these patterns requires careful listening and learning.

CLOCK-ORIENTED VS. TASK-ORIENTED VS. RELATIONAL TIME ORIENTATION: The "time orientation" of the dominant North American culture is highly "clock-oriented" and sometimes "task oriented." Events (including meetings and sporting events) start at a specific time, and those not present at that time are "late." Events finish either based on a running clock (basketball), a series of specific, ordered events (In baseball, eighteen alternating half-innings of three outs each) or some combination of the two (as in football, where the running of the clock is highly dependent on a sequence of specific tasks). Much of the North American business and education worlds operate this way. However, many global cultures and North American subcultures have a far more "relational" time orientation, where things begin and end based on relationships between individuals of differing status. Sports follow a clock-oriented time dynamic if practice ends "at 7:30," and a relational time orientation if practices ends "when the coach says it's over." Practice might end when a key player walks off the field, with or without verbal announcement, either because a coach has delegated this authority to a team captain, or because that player has more social influence than the coach. As with the example of the athlete helping his grandmother with groceries, other community members may be considered to have more social status than those who run the league; the athlete may prefer to be on time to practice, but it is not socially acceptable to refuse a request from an older relative until that relative releases him from responsibility. Based on their relationship and status, "I have to go to practice now" is not an "excuse" to end the "task" that collective family responsibility currently requires. In nearly every sporting event, the game will begin without an athlete who is "late," and that athlete may not play at all. But in some contexts, including some community baseball and basketball leagues, it would be considered improper to start the game "before everyone gets there," which reflects a more relational time dynamic, as well as a more collectivist orientation. Those of us who coach and mentor in distressed communities will usually need to learn and respect the habitual time orientations of the community we serve (which can vary widely according to circumstance), rather than impose our own—while we may think we are "teaching responsibility" by emphasizing a highly clock-oriented time dynamic, doing so in a community that is not typically oriented this way will have a negative impact on our success and acceptance in the long run if it interferes with other important dynamics.

MONEY: Money is a delicate topic in most cultures. Community development efforts typically take place in poorer neighborhoods, where many people experience financial difficulties and challenges. It can be a real challenge to financially sustain a sports league, while remaining sensitive to how our neighbors might respond based on their ability or inability to pay. In some contexts, it may be acceptable to require everyone to pay in order to participate. If some people will have their fee waived, it may be better to keep this fairly private, or it may be fine to make a simple public announcement to ask for help if it is needed. Some may withdraw rather than ask for help. Cultural values can shape the expectations of what influence donors might expect to have based on the money they give toward an organization. In our experience, many sports programs in distressed communities are unable to secure fees from many of their participants without creating unwanted social tension, and many people will avoid discussing finances if they can, which can be very frustrating in the beginning. Each community needs to give careful thought and prayer to making their sports-related programs and resources available to their most vulnerable young people.

AUTHORITY: Views on authority can vary widely by culture. Some cultures place more respect in academic degrees or in personal experience. Some cultures value democratic affirmation of leadership; some sports teams may frequently hold "votes" on issues of moderate importance to create buy-in from athletes. Others may place more value in expertise and delegation, and buy-in may come from assigning tasks to players and praising the results. Part of the success of sports as a Christian Community Development tool comes from the fact that coaches are held in high esteem by young people in most parts of North America. Still, cultural expectations of a person in authority will vary by local culture. Do people expect the person in charge to be warm, and lead relationally? Or to be distant, to avoid relational awkwardness or the appearance of favoritism? Again, there is no simple recipe for success; leaders must listen carefully to representative voices in order to discern how to be true to themselves while also meeting the cultural expectations of the community.

These are just a few cultural areas where questions typically arise in community-development-based sports ministry. There are plenty of dynamics to understand about cultural competence. Cultures can be "low context," where people are expected to say quickly and directly what they mean (think of a sandlot baseball game in Chicago) "high context," where dropping hints and reading cues is important (think of a charity gala on the Philadelphia mainline). Cultures can deal with wrongdoing by emphasizing guilt (what will you do to make it right?) or shame (what will you do to prove yourself again?). Acquiring cultural competence is an important and complicated process, and we encourage anyone working in community-development-related sports ministry to seek out these skills.

But while knowledge can go a long way, it can't replace the simple, respectful act of listening and learning. Ask questions instead of suggesting answers right away. When conflict emerges, instead of asking "Who is in the wrong?" ask, "What made each of us react the way we did?" Being aware of preconceived ideas is important; if we go into a situation with preconceived answers, we often end up selectively listening for ideas that confirm those answers. Accountability is an important part of listening; leaders should have some kind of system in place that makes them accountable to listen to others, and accountable for what they do with what they learn.

And while talk of culture in North America is often framed in terms of cultural conflict or unforgivable social errors, artist Makoto Fujimura (2017) writes: "Culture is not a territory to be won or lost but a resource we are called to steward with care. Culture is a garden to be cultivated" (40). A core task of community development is working together to *build* a thriving culture, where neighbors cooperate to create a community where everyone can both contribute and receive, and where the divisions that characterize human life are superseded by the interdependence for which God designed us.

To build a thriving neighborhood culture requires us to understand the history that has shaped our neighbors and our neighborhood, and to act on that understanding. The challenges that those who work in Christian Community Development seek to tackle do not emerge on their own; things like poverty and violence are born out of the divisions produced by human sin and selfishness and require a kind of healing that only the Lord can provide. This brings us to the next key principle of Christian Community Development: *Reconciliation.*

Reconciliation: Coming Together

The pursuit of *reconciliation* is fundamental to building healthy communities. Many of the visible and invisible problems in our neighborhoods have come about because of division and exclusion, and to restore our struggling neighborhoods, we must find ways to bring together people, and groups of people, who have been driven apart. The CCD concept of reconciliation has two parts: reconciliation of people to God, and reconciliation of people to people.

Reconciliation of people to God is traditionally called *evangelism* or *sharing the gospel*, delivering the good news of salvation through the sacrifice on the cross of Jesus Christ the Son of God, and his resurrection after three days. Through making a decision to accept Jesus Christ as Lord, we become *reconciled* to God, and begin a relationship with Jesus Christ that lasts throughout this life and for an eternity with God in Heaven. Evangelism is a spiritual gift given to some (Ephesians 4:11) but is also the responsibility of all followers of Jesus Christ (Matthew 28:19).

Sports ministry has a long and successful tradition of evangelism. The Fellowship of Christian Athletes (FCA) was founded on the idea that if athletes could be hired to sell products for corporations, they could just as easily and convincingly present the gospel of Jesus Christ to the world. Millions of people have become followers of Jesus through FCA and ministries like it. Sports ministry has been making a powerful evangelistic impact for decades and continues to do so every day.

Jeff Biddle recalls an evangelistic movement among athletes in Charleston:

> We saw a powerful evangelistic movement when high school football and basketball players prepared their friends, one by one, to receive the gospel of Jesus Christ. Some of the young men who were strongest in their faith would talk to their teammates for a period of time until it seemed like they were ready—then, in a funny sort of tradition, would bring them to a Chinese restaurant, and we would invite them to make the decision to follow Christ. The team became a network of trust through which the young men who were following Jesus built relationships with their teammates and passed on the gospel message.

Dorian Etheridge, who now plays linebacker for the Louisville Cardinals, recalls being a part of that movement:

> Growing up I was always a good football player, I had a lot of friends, I had a good home life and everything, but there was always something missing. As I grew up, it was like that hole was getting bigger and bigger, and I was wondering what it was. I started making new friends and everything, and just reaching out to people, I started working harder in school, even in sports, but that hole was still there.
>
> When you're on a team playing football, the relationships you build, you get so close you call each other brothers. When you become that close you just trust somebody more. In my situation I wasn't that close with God but being on the team let me open up to my teammates. I saw they were going to church and everything, and they invited me. I went with them, and it was like—that's what it was. I just knew then. It was God that was missing in my life the whole time.
>
> A friend can introduce you to God just like a pastor would. my friends were fifteen years old when they did it. It might sound far-fetched, but in reality, that's how it really happened. I saw that change me so much, it was just right. It's hard to submit yourself to God that young, but I feel like I did it, because I had friends who could do it.

Accepting the lordship of Jesus Christ is about more than our eternal destiny. When we accept the invitation to follow Jesus Christ and become Christians, we become citizens of God's Kingdom, welcomed into the forgiveness, wholeness, mercy and justice that God has always intended for His people, and we are called to pursue a life that reflects that reality here on Earth.

That means that once we have been reconciled to God, we also start being reconciled to one another. The second great commandment of Christ is to love our neighbors as ourselves, but the world is full of hurts and grief and divisions that hold people back from doing that. In any community, as we get to know our neighbors, we realize that a long history of unresolved sins, wounds, attitudes, and injustices keeps people from loving each other the way Jesus intended.

But once we have caught a glimpse of the heavenly reality of Christ, we are able to *imagine* a world where relationships are based on forgiveness, where neighbors love one another, and where people contribute freely to each other's well-being. The Bible frequently refers to this reality with the Hebrew word *Shalom*. This word is usually translated into English as "peace," but it means much more than that. Bruce Bradshaw (1993), in his book *Bringing the Gap: Evangelism, Development, and Shalom* writes: "[T]he concept of *shalom* means more than the mere absence of war, our common definition of peace. Instead, *shalom* is a concept that communicates the sense of 'human welfare, health, and well-being, in both spiritual and physical aspects.' *Shalom* is a way of life that characterizes the covenant relationship between God and his people" (17). The concept of *Shalom* helps us define the goals and vision of Christian Community Development. Sports are an excellent platform for evangelism; they are also an excellent tool for the long-term project of building *shalom* within a community.

Sports and Shalom

The Hebrew concept of *Shalom* implies wholeness, completeness, the sense that everything is taken care of, a lack of fear and worry, the presence of justice, a sense of "holistic peace." Shalom is the whole family around the Christmas dinner table: everyone is there, and no one is missing, there is enough to go around, and everyone is full of a holy sort of joy. Shalom is the neighborhood picnic: everyone was invited, and everyone brought something to share; the children are playing, the elders are smiling, and people are having too much fun to notice the sun sinking in the sky. Shalom is the high school football game: an electric atmosphere of bright lights and bright colors, young people on the field playing their roles with energy, challenging yet respecting their opponents, fans cheering for their children and their classmates, smiling people moving between pockets of conversation, catching up on the highs and lows of daily life from the past week.

Shalom may be hard to define, but for many athletes, it isn't hard to understand. For many young people, sports *is* their picture of shalom, their place of active, constructive peace. Sports is their safe place, their meaningful pursuit, where they know they belong, where they have a role to play, where they will be praised when they succeed, and forgiven and allowed a chance to improve when they come up short. For many athletes, sports are one of the first places in their life where they find shared purpose, where they learn to celebrate the joy of victory, and turn defeats into chances to learn and improve. Countless young athletes find a life-defining brotherhood and sisterhood on their sports teams. The sense of purpose, the sense of contribution, the sense of teamwork, the sense of community belonging, the sense of growth and success and learning from failure that make up the best of the sports experience are pieces of what makes up of *shalom*, part of experiencing what God our Father created us for.

This is especially true for many young people struggling to build a sense of self and a hope for the future in our distressed communities. For those whose lives can seem unstable and unpredictable, the world of sports provides structure and rewards. For those who through have come to question their worth, their role, and their place in the world, the world of sports offers defined roles and contributions that are valued by the whole. For those who experience homes, streets, and schools where they feel unsafe and unprotected, the world of sports offers a safe place to escape to. For those who have experienced drastic consequences from small mistakes, whether in the street or in overly punitive schools, the world of sports offers a chance to learn from mistakes and grow, instead of being crushed by punishments. For those tempted to find "belonging" in unhealthy places like gangs or abusive dependencies, the world of sports offers a liberating sense of belonging in shared accomplishment and hard work.

Many of our young people have flocked to athletic fields for all the right reasons—because there, they begin to find a picture of the peace, acceptance, wholeness, and purpose that God has always intended for them. This is a big part of what makes sports such an incredible tool for Christian Community Development. When we harness this reality and translate it back into the life of the community in meaningful ways, the impact is enormous.

Sports, Violence, and Conflict Resolution

Violence exists everywhere, but in our distressed communities, violence presents itself in especially obvious and destructive ways, and many of our young people have grown up with experiences of fearing for their physical safety. A lot of this violence is interpersonal, from domestic violence to gang clashes to unresolved interpersonal feuds to random acts of cruelty stemming from uncontrolled anger and pain. The deepest roots of these problems are often found in institutional forms of violence, including the abuse of state-sanctioned power by police and other authorities, incarceration, and institutional systems that deprive people of their basic needs and rights.

Those of us who live and work in such environments can become overwhelmed by the tragic of cycles of anger, violence, and deprivation. Most of us have encountered young people who, through exposure to violence, stress, trauma, or a lack of boundaries, have become "short-fused" and prone to losing emotional control—these young people can be challenging to work with and difficult to help, and have usually experienced rejection from adults who find them too troubling to deal with. Punitive systems that deal harshly with their behavior only compound the problem, casting a threatening cloud over their futures. On the street, the consequences of unregulated outbursts can be deadly. Although disruptive behavior can't be ignored, neither should it be a reason to reject a young person. Helping our youth transform their behavior and escape a cycle of anger and violence is essential to helping our communities transform. But in communities with few resources, the right environment and support to help these young people to change can be hard to come by.

Once again, our sports programs are often perfectly positioned to provide such an environment. For many of our young people, sports teams are a temporary haven from a dangerous world, and a place to safely let off steam from anger and aggression that has built up over time. If we are intentional about what we do, we can use this safe haven as a place to train young people in emotional self-regulation and conflict management, turning sports into an incredibly effective tool for healing cycles of personal and community violence. The structure that many sports provide—safe and healthy aggression, close contact with mature adults, cooperation and team-building—can be combined with the right set of experiences and the right mentoring to make our sports programs the perfect context to give young people the tools to deal with anger, violence, and conflict resolution, equipping them to build a very different future for themselves and for their community.

In Baltimore, Jeff Thompson teaches the athletes of 10:12 Sports that sports are a "dress rehearsal" for real life:

> I tell them, "make mistakes and fix them here, before you make mistakes in the street and somebody gets hurt." This invitation has led to the field and the court being places to grieve and express the trauma that has been bottled up because of the lack of perceived "safe spaces" for our teens in their environments. This shows itself when a simple mistake or bad call can lead to a meltdown, and trigger grief. It's obvious that the source of that meltdown goes far beyond what has happened in that game. For us, part of the reconciliation process has been an increased emphasis on learning more about trauma-informed care (something we will discuss more in Chapter 7), looking at how better to create spaces where our young men can grieve and express themselves, and to be better prepared to walk with them through that.
>
> We've also started to implement something called "restorative circles" at the end of the game, where guys can encourage each other and say what's on their minds, while other teens around hear and see them in a circle, we lock hands and join in prayer to end that time, emphasizing the reality of sticking together as a community.
>
> We've also implemented something called "league night" which is a safe place for the whole league to come together every week. We eat together and enjoy one another watching football clips, playing

games and being active. This has become a place where lots of teens involved in the league get to hang and bond with various teens from other West Baltimore neighborhoods that they wouldn't typically hang out with. As prevalent as violence is in our West Baltimore communities, this kind of safe space and these kinds of bonds go a long way toward reducing and resolving conflict.

In order to teach reconciliation through sports, we have to be intentional about how we handle certain moments. Chris Lahr remembers a time when a conflict broke out that could have been disastrous for the program as a whole, but instead turned out to be a moment of growth for everyone:

> One reality of running a sports program is that you have to fund it. One of our funders wanted to visit one of the teams to see us in action. That was a no brainer—I would have her come to my practice, as we ran a tight practice, there was never drama, and I had a few youth she could talk to in the process of her visit. Shortly after she arrived, I walked her to the middle of the field to observe. As she started talking to one of of the youth, the first fight ever to break out at one of my practices erupted. The fight was between three guys in a triad battle. Then there was Josh, a leader on the team—he just about lost it as he saw his three friends fight. He was close to all three guys and he started yelling, and the scene quickly turned to chaos. We were able to split the three fighters and I went over to Josh to talk with him.
>
> Before I could say a thing, he stated he was sorry for getting so angry but that he couldn't handle seeing three of his close friends fighting and that Timoteo was not a place for that. I told him that this could be a moment to allow his leadership to shine, that he was the glue to bring these three broken pieces back together. He got up and went to each of the three friends, and he "squashed the

beef" they had. The three parties, Josh, and the whole team gathered. Josh had a few words of encouragement for the three and the team. He then asked me to pray for the team, and we did so right there on the field. Practice resumed, the unity became a reality, and the violence truly stopped right there. There was no revenge, no getting your people, no grabbing a gun. A fight occurred, but peace won the day and a peer leader took a step up.

Especially with a key supporter watching, it could have been tempting to respond to Josh harshly for not "rising above" what happened or setting a better example. Instead, Chris was able to engage a budding leader in a process of reconciliation in a way that demonstrated what this sports program was capable of doing for the community as a whole. Teaching reconciliation through sports requires real patience and dedication. As coaches and mentors, we have to pay close attention to certain moments of emotion and conflict, and have the emotional maturity not to be drawn in. We have to be aware of the capabilities of key young leaders, and trust and empower them to create solutions on their own, rather than imposing our own more heavy-handed authority. On a personal level, we need to develop our own understanding of conflict resolution in order to be able to pass it along to younger people.

When we are able to do these things, sports can become an essential, low-stakes way for young people to safely train themselves under the guidance of trusted mentors to handle peak emotions and resolve conflicts. When we train our athletes to do this, we are training them in an art that will promote *reconciliation* in their relationships for the rest of their lives. And when sports programs are community-rooted, those reconciled relationships begin to impact the community as a whole. Not only do athletes apply the conflict resolution skills learned on the field to their lives in the community, but when young people who have had conflict with one another in the past are drawn into a common goal and purpose in the world of sports, they form new bonds that motivate them to overcome past divisions and move forward together. When sports programs bring diverse people into proximity with shared goals, bridges are built and social ties are strengthened, building a greater potential for lasting, thriving peace within the community.

In Baltimore, Jeff Thompson saw the reconciliation that his young men learned through 10:12 sports extend into the neighborhood once they began to realize what they were capable of:

When I asked one of my young men what kept him involved in 10:12 sports, he told me, "There's not a lot of beef that happens out here, and I like that." 10:12 was clearly a place he felt safe and welcome, as opposed to many spaces in our community.

I'm also reminded how one of my young men, on the first year of the league, pointed out a group of kids from another team and said that they were part of the guys that they had beef with and had fought with (crew against crew). The league had eventually turned into a place where everyone contributed in creating a safe space, which they owned, and continue to own, setting an example for younger boys.

There are never fights on game day. It's a hundred young men in one place, and that says something about the space that they have created and what they value—they value peace. They've all agreed, there's so much beef in so many places that they all have to watch their backs off the field, so let's make sure this isn't a place where anyone has to do that.

My encouragement to them is always that *they* created that safe space of peace, reconciliation, and brotherhood at our program, and that it's not something that has to just stay at the field or court but rather something that they can create in other spaces—if they did it here, they can do it again.

We've also had the chance to encourage a unique violence prevention initiative that one of our young men, Daquan Mints, has created, called "Guns Down, Gloves Up." It's an initiative to encourage people with beef to put on gloves and box it out, rather than taking it to somewhere that would involve guns. He actually has different places in the neighborhood where people have the gloves ready, and people can arrange to box rather than escalate to something that's more violent. He made t-shirts that we helped him promote and encouraged people to support his movement. In this case, the sport turns actual beef, that could have escalated into someone being shot, into something that can be hashed out and left behind. It can be controversial, in that some people say, "I'm not for fighting at all." But we encouraged our community to get behind it. If you can take a real problem, and turn it into a boxing match, and everyone walks away with their life, that's solving a very real problem of youth violence in our neighborhood.

In 1 Corinthians 5:16-21, the Apostle Paul describes how our own reconciliation to God transforms us into "ambassadors of reconciliation," helping to bring the world into harmony with God's purposes:

> So from now on we regard no one from a worldly point of view. Though we once regarded Christ in this way, we do so no longer. Therefore, if anyone is in Christ, the new creation has come: The old has gone, the new is here! All this is from God, who reconciled us to himself through Christ and gave us the ministry of reconciliation: that God was reconciling the world to himself in Christ, not counting people's sins against them. And he has committed to us the message of reconciliation. We are therefore Christ's ambassadors, as though God were making his appeal through us. We implore you on Christ's behalf: Be reconciled to God. God made him who had no sin to be sin for us, so that in him we might become the righteousness of God.

Our sports programs afford us the amazing opportunity to train and empower "ambassadors of reconciliation," who will make our communities safer, more peaceful places, places where people can experience the *shalom* that God intended for His people.

Sports and Restorative Justice

God's *shalom* is not merely the absence of conflict; it is also the presence of justice. In many of our distressed communities, justice has been perverted in two common ways: by favoring those with wealth and power, which can lead quickly to a mistrust of institutional justice, and by an extreme focus on *retribution,* or punishing offenders for the sake of punishment or deterrence itself.

Draconian and corrupt policing practices have long been applied to distressed communities in the United States, especially communities of color. Law professor Michelle Alexander (2012), author of *The New Jim Crow,* describes how in the last few decades, an escalating "war on drugs" and associated policies have resulted in long prison sentences removing young and middle-aged men from communities for years at a time, and criminal records excluding staggering numbers from employment and housing, a phenomenon collectively referred to as *mass incarceration*. Many of these are only "guilty" of being addicts, or of being loosely associated with others who have committed more serious crimes; in some places it is difficult to maintain community ties to friends and family at all without being criminalized. The United States, with only 5% of the world's population, now has 25% of the world's prisoners, drawn primarily from its low-income neighborhoods. Highly retributive justice policies have become a community-defining crisis for the specific North American communities they have targeted. When we coach and mentor athletes in distressed communities, we can be almost certain that their lives have been affected by retributive justice and mass incarceration. They have watched, feeling helpless, as neighbors, family members, or parents have been removed from their lives for years at a time with no appeal; they have seen older family members harassed, handcuffed and intentionally humiliated, or experienced this themselves.

Scholars such as Dr. William Ayers (2001) in his book *Zero Tolerance: Resisting the Drive for Punishment in Our Schools* and Dr. Victor Rios (2011) in his book *Punished: Policing the Lives of Black and Latino Boys* document how these policies target young people, especially young men, from an early age. A "zero tolerance" approach to school discipline, that emphasizes suspension and expulsion of students judged to be a "risk," has been applied primarily to students of color and students from poorer communities. Close connections between the educational and criminal justice systems have created a "school-to-prison pipeline" that moves certain young people toward incarceration and other forms of state-based control and retributive punishment from an early age. Many of our athletes have for years attended schools whose fear-based discipline policies communicate a chilling message: "Measure up or be cast out. You are of value only if you meet the standard, and if you fall short, your hopes for the future may be cut off at any moment. There are few second chances, so don't blow it." Many of us have watched in distress as a punitive system derails young people's lives over the small kinds of mistakes and indiscretions that characterize teenage life. As we watch these traumas unfold in the lives of our athletes, it can be easy to wonder: what could organized sports possibly do to help with such a complex set of issues? One answer is found in modeling an alternative Christian tradition called *Restorative Justice.*

Retributive justice is about punishing offenders; it does almost nothing for victims of crime and often harms the offenders themselves far beyond what they deserve. *Restorative justice* is about restoring both the *offender* and the *victim* to wholeness. The North American tradition of restorative justice emerged from the historic peace churches: Mennonites, Quakers, and others who fled religious persecution in Europe to create small, tight-knit Christian communities in North America, communities which placed an emphasis on pursuing restoration and reconciliation when a member violated community standards. As Dr. Howard Zehr (2015), a Mennonite writer and criminologist, puts it: "Biblical Justice...is in fact an act of love that seeks to make things right. Love and Justice are not opposites, nor are they in conflict. Instead, love provides for a justice that seeks to make right." Zehr (2015) defines the "restorative justice paradigm" this way: "Crime is a violation of people and relationships. It creates obligations to make things right. Justice involves the victim, the offender, and the community in search for solutions which promote repair, reconciliation, and reassurance" (183). When standards or trust have been broken, restorative Justice asks the fundamental question, "what can we do to make this right?"

Many of our athletes have seen their lives and the lives of those in their community damaged or destroyed by a draconian, retributive form of "justice." Coaching and mentoring them well requires a sensitivity to the role that transgression and punishment has played in their lives. When we apply restorative practices, our sports programs can offer these young people an incredibly liberating experience of being included, supported and restored in spite of their mistakes—an experience that can be hard to come by in the other institutions available to them. This experience of being accepted and restored can be life-changing, empowering their sense of self-worth, and giving them tools to handle mistakes and conflict in the future.

Team sports require a team cohesion that is more an art than a science. Athletes play different roles within the team beyond their athletic roles, as social leaders, peacemakers, and encouragers—or as disruptors, slackers, or instigators. Athletes will from time-to-time violate team standards, in ways that are easy to measure (missing practice, or blowing up at the coach), in ways that are directly related to game play (hogging the ball or committing a penalty that costs the team the game), or in ways that are more difficult to pin down (belittling the contribution of younger players, or lacking discipline in practice). Bringing restorative practices to sports begins with asking the question in any of these situations: "What can we do to make this right?" How can the offending athlete move forward in a constructive way? How can those hurt by his behavior be made whole? What can different members of the team contribute to this process? Many of us recall moments in the locker room when a team captain made a spontaneous speech after a loss holding teammates accountable to do better, or when a quarterback made a specific effort to encourage and restore a receiver who dropped a pass. These were moments of *restoration*, and skilled coaches and mentors can engage and encourage this restoration in a way that holds athletes accountable for their actions, but teaches them to cooperate in providing a constructive way forward, by *identifying* the problem, *creating* a path to restoration, *equipping* athletes and adult leaders to pursue that path, and *welcoming* everyone to full participation in a new, better dynamic.

Timoteo Sports has seen firsthand how sports can contribute to the restoration of young people who are going astray:

> Timoteo has given us plenty of examples of restorative justice over the years. Henry is one of those examples. We have known Henry since he was a baby, and as a small child he found himself on the Timoteo field watching his older brother play. Henry was a "Timoteo kid" through and through, and as soon as he was old enough, he joined the team. Initially he did not play a lot, but as he grew, so did his talents—and his attitude. At the age of 16 he was in his last year of summer camp, and we had to kick him out because of his attitude, dirty hits, and excessive foul mouth. He was devastated that we actually kicked him out, but we were relieved! We loved Henry, and we knew Henry would come back around start of the next season, but we felt this was the best move for him and the camp.
>
> Fast forward seven months to the start of the Timoteo season, when we began advertising for youth coaches for the next summer

camp. Lo and behold, Henry was old enough and wanted to be a summer camp coach! Initially we laughed, but we could not deny the seriousness in his face and tone of voice. So we made him work for the position—we said if he walked out on his Timoteo team even once this season we would not consider him for the coaching position. We made it clear that he had to clean up the language and be "Mr. Team Player" this year for his squad. We were absolutely shocked at Henry's turnaround! He was a new kid, a leader, a team player, and ready to be a summer camp coach.

We put the call out for summer camp coaches, and sure enough, Henry's application came in. Within a few weeks we held interviews and we were all impressed with his maturity and growth in just a few short months. Then came time to announce the new coaches...We let everyone know they got the position except Henry. He wanted it so bad, and we received multiple texts from him inquiring whether or not he got accepted. We made him sweat for a few days, stating we were debating between him and someone else, the whole time knowing he was going to be accepted. Sometimes restorative justice comes with pain. We asked him to send us a final message as to why he should be made a coach. This is what he wrote (yes, this was the longest text I have ever received):

> I want this job because I feel like it would help me mature more as a young man and it would also teach me to keep my head up even when things are hard and when u come across kids that are hard to deal with. And I got a feeling that at the end of the summer camp I can change some of these kids lives and I want to grow a bond with all the players and I also want every kid and coach there to feel like they can come to me for anything because I'll be there. That's what family is for and in my past years participating in summer camp and even in regular Timoteo I learned that we are all family and that you can always call somebody from Timoteo for anything and they'll try their best to help you. I want to also learn how to manage my money and I think this can help me overall. I also think that summer camp will change my life like Timoteo as a whole already has.
>
> I know that I have gotten into some messed up situations that I really regret but I have shown some really good improvements during this year with being a leader and a captain and not getting in trouble on the field and keeping my head up at the lowest of times and the losses and keeping my head up when we are winning. I also learned how to encourage my teammates to do better on and off the field because like I said

we are all family. I was never late to practice or any games and I always led by example.

Henry got the job! Not only did he get the job, but he excelled and continues to act as a peer leader in our community. Henry's story shows that it doesn't take long for someone to make significant changes in their life.

Another example comes from a young man named Zeus. For several years Timoteo ran an adult flag football league in the fall for our alumni and others connected to them. This league was a little different as it was more physical than our youth league as we allowed blocking and stiff arms. In the course of a game Zeus, an offensive lineman, lost all control. Zeus is a big man, and up to that point, I had never seen anyone get so angry (except maybe my wife one time...). It was as if he turned into another person as he literally pulled a freshly planted tree from the ground and he started foaming at the mouth. Eventually a couple of us were able to settle him down and bring him back to reality.

The season came to an end, and before we knew it, the new season was upon us. Zeus showed up, and he seemed determined to turn over a new leaf. Each week he was the first to the field and the last to leave as he helped the staff set up and tear down each week. Halfway through the season Zeus and I were talking, and he asked if I thought he was different. I told him he seemed more at peace, and the trees in the neighborhood were thankful for that. He said he had talked to a local pastor that often visited the games and he told Zeus he saw a change. Zeus went on to say that it was something about Timoteo that causes people to change, to grow, to be restored.

A big part of that "something" is a restorative attitude that focuses on helping people grow, move forward, and fix mistakes instead of focusing on punishment. Blending restorative practices into our sports programs can be incredibly challenging. It can draw criticism from those who believe in a "tough" approach, it requires buy-in from athletes whose first inclination may not be to pursue forgiveness or restoration, and it requires emotional strength on the part of the leaders. But in our sports programs, we have an opportunity to imitate Christ by modeling and teaching a form of reconciliation that is desperately needed in our communities. The experience for our athletes is in turn incredibly transformative. Young people who have come to expect rejection based on the smallest transgressions experience restoration instead, which instills hope and opens the door to the gospel of Jesus Christ through a powerful experience of grace.

As coaches and mentors in community-rooted programs, we also have the opportunity to be part of restorative justice in the wider community, by participating in the restoration of our athletes when they violate community standards beyond the program itself; we discuss one example of this in Dr. Scott N. Brooks's research in Chapter Six. When we coach and mentor in distressed communities, we will certainly see our athletes caught up in damaging behaviors or false accusations that lead to punishments that could potentially cripple their futures. Pursuing restorative justice requires the involvement of the community as a whole, people who will both hold the young person accountable, and provide the expertise, connections, support, and advocacy necessary to secure positive outcomes within corrupt systems, something we will talk more about in Chapter Nine. The more strong, positive, community-based relationships a young person has, the more likely their outcomes will be restorative.

Sports and Racial Reconciliation

Christian Community Development emphasizes reconciliation to God through the good news of Jesus Christ, and reconciliation between people who have been at odds with one another. But reconciliation does not stop there—reconciliation also involves people groups who have historically been divided socially and culturally pursuing the difficult task of coming together to form a common, communal life. Christian Community Development has its origins in the American Civil Rights Movement. Dr. John Perkins (2007) first committed himself to reconciliation after he and others were beaten and tortured inside a police station in Brandon, Mississippi:

> For the first time, I saw what hate had done to those people. These policemen were poor. They saw themselves as failures. The only way they knew how to find a sense of worth was by beating us. Their racism made them feel like 'somebody.' When I saw that, I just couldn't hate back. I could only pity them. I said to God that night. 'God, if You will let me get out of this jail alive'—and I really didn't think I would, maybe I was trying to bargain with Him—'I really want to preach a gospel that will heal these people, too.' (pg. 107-108).

With this bold act of forgiveness, Dr. Perkins began a lifetime of preaching racial reconciliation.

While forgiveness and reconciliation between two opposing parties can be easy to understand and model, reconciliation between people groups is a large-scale challenge that requires spiritual and cultural leadership, an ongoing mission that remains unresolved over the past 400 years in North America. But without this part of the mission, our communities cannot be made whole. Even in communities where the main divide is not between black and white neighbors, there will nearly always be a history of division and social and economic disadvantage that have contributed to the community's distress, and a need for group reconciliation in order for the community to thrive. The first step is to listen carefully to the community to learn where those divisions lie.

In North America, the sports world has historically been a unique and important space in which racial progress has been worked out over time; many of us are familiar with some of the landmark moments. Record setting track athlete Jesse Owens made a bold statement with his victories at the Nazi-run 1934 Berlin Olympics. Before the Brown vs. Board of Education ruling integrated American schools, Jackie Robinson integrated Major League Baseball in 1947. Texas Western College won an NCAA Basketball championship with an all-black starting lineup in the midst of growing civil rights tensions in 1966. Social and political statements, from the raised fists of Tommie Smith and John Carlos at the 1968 Olympics to the kneeling of Colin Kaepernick during the National Anthem at NFL games in 2016, have brought issues of racial justice to the forefront of conversation in the sports world. Racial bias and disparity continue to linger in obvious ways, including the troublingly small number of Black coaches and quarterbacks in the majority-Black NFL and NBA.

Signposts like these mark out the way in which the sports world has often mirrored North American culture with a story of hard-fought, tumultuous integration, with key moments of victory, observable progress, and lingering disparities reflecting structural injustices. As it has for decades, the sports world continues to play a significant role as a space of encounter and integration across racial and economic lines. If we are careless, our sports programs will likely reinforce the structural biases of the culture around us. But certain aspects of the team sport experience lend themselves to creating spaces where reconciliation can take place.

Most of us who coach and mentor athletes in distressed communities can immediately identify racial dynamics at play in our programs. Does the population of the program reflect the population of the community? Do athletes of certain ethnicities gravitate toward certain sports, or certain roles within those sports? Are most of our athletes from a single ethnicity, but the adult staff and volunteers diverse? Are the athletes diverse, and most of the adults white? Do referees or other people in authority seem to react differently to white athletes and athletes of color? To what degree are youth sports considered part of holistic youth development? A path toward success in life? A recreational service "experience" being offered at a price? Simple answers to these, as well as much deeper questions, will likely reveal racial, ethnic, and cultural dynamics affecting the program.

While not every ethnic or racial disparity is cause for concern—we may not need to wring our hands if recent Central American immigrants to Minneapolis are playing more soccer and less hockey than the city average—acknowledgement and handling of the racial and ethnic dynamics in our programs requires the kind of cultural sensitivity and awareness described in Chapter Two, and an intentionality about upholding God's heavenly vision as described in Revelation 7:9 of "every tribe, nation, people and tongue" praising the Lord together. This vision which requires us to go against the grain of North American culture as a whole. If we are aware and intentional, certain aspects of youth sports help us create an excellent environment for cross-cultural encounter and reconciliation.

Many sports programs in racially diverse communities create a space for *proximity* between athletes of different ethnic backgrounds. Even in communities with a relatively high degree of social segregation, school and community teams in popular sports are often diverse spaces, where young people are given the opportunity to meet and comingle with people of very different backgrounds. Proximity is an important first step toward community reconciliation. As Michelle Warren (2017), CCDA's Advocacy and Strategic Engagement Director, writes, "The longer we stay proximate, the more our perspective is shaped and the more we respond to what needs to be changed. Proximity is transformational. It unearths the rules of our social construct and levels the playing field enough that we are able to journey with those impacted by injustice in deeply shared ways" (18).

Proximity, however, is only a first step. How we choose to handle being around people who have different backgrounds makes the difference between reinforcing the status quo and moving toward reconciliation. Other key aspects of the team sport experience help us make that move.

The nature of many sports—where the fastest, strongest, most talented, most motivated person is likely to win, regardless of their background or culture—has helped make the sports world a frontier of racial integration. This is not to say that racial bias cannot influence outcomes in the sports world—even social dynamics as simple as whose father sponsored the team jerseys can impact who is chosen to play pitcher or quarterback—but pioneers like Jackie Robinson were able to overcome both barriers and stereotypes because their sport allowed them to demonstrate their capabilities with their performance record. The more we ensure that the distribution and acknowledgement of talent on our teams is fair, the more we contribute to an environment where young people learn to work together alongside those of different backgrounds, acknowledging their strengths and contributions along with their own.

When young athletes are brought into proximity with one another, and the environment is meritocratic and fair, team sports offer a complex and emotionally intense *shared experience* that forms deep, lifelong bonds, bonds that help to overcome prejudices and produce community reconciliation. Sports psychologists are developing a growing understanding of the social science and even the brain science behind these bonds. Participating in a team sport, playing a role and making a contribution to shared goals plays a key role in adolescent socialization and development. Participating together creates moments of collective excitement, brains coursing with cortisol (the stress hormone) and adrenaline (the exertion hormone), where dependence on one another leads to triumph, triggering a release of dopamine (the joy hormone), literally "brain-washes" the developing adolescent mind, programming it to connect its own joy success with that of teammates. When teammates are of diverse backgrounds, this lays a lifelong framework for reaching across those divides with the expectation of shared success. A wise coach or mentor can harness that experience and give it social meaning, helping her athletes understand the sense of the importance and implications of their shared bonds of trust, and to apply those bonds in a constructive way within the community.

Many forms of athletic competition also provide a *collective local experience* both for the team, and for the families of the community. The team is associated with a specific school, neighborhood, or city, and the jerseys bear their colors. The triumph of the team is a collective triumph for teammates, for their families, for alumni, and for friends, sponsors, and other supporters. This collective local experience in turn places the athletes themselves in a cherished place within the community. An athlete from an otherwise marginalized background will experience having their contribution valued and affirmed at an exciting community event.

Team sports offer us an excellent framework for promoting and facilitating reconciliation, but to take advantage of that opportunity requires leadership that is intentional and often difficult. Once the proximity and collective experience of team sports leads to cross-cultural relationships, we need to decide how to handle and frame the meaning of those experiences. Dr. Brenda Salter McNeil (2015), Professor of Reconciliation Studies at Seattle Pacific University, outlines in her book, *Roadmap to Reconciliation* how many multiethnic organizations experience *cataclysmic events*, cross-cultural moments that produce a strong response. This could be an ethnically based cultural conflict within the organization, an incident involving overt racism, or a reaction to a national event with racial or ethnic significance, like Colin Kaepernick's protests, which elicited local responses in teams and schools around the country. It is not these events themselves, but the way we choose to respond, that determines whether the organization returns to the status quo, or moves forward in reconciliation.

Once a cataclysmic event occurs, cross-cultural relationships are strained, and conflict often emerges, which may manifest itself as forms of overt tension or silent withdrawal. If the people experiencing the conflict are willing to stay open and persist, a *realization* phase begins, in which people allow their cross-cultural relationships to inform them about a new reality. If they embrace that reality, they enter a phase that Dr. McNeil calls *your people become my people,* named after Ruth's statement to Naomi in the Bible. One of the reasons team sports can work so well to facilitate experiences of reconciliation is that the team itself, as well as the community that supports it, create a shared identity framework that makes it easier for athletes to embrace those from other cultures as *my people*. However, this process requires intentional respect and communication as its implications are realized. Once the group has chosen to continue journeying together, *preparation* for facing the new reality begins, and finally, *activation* puts the group into action, pursuing reconciliation together.

Jeff Biddle recalls a series of events surrounding the majority-Black football and basketball teams at Capital High School in mostly white West Virginia, and the way key leaders used those events to bring young people together across racial and cultural lines:

In Charleston, one of our "cataclysmic events" came when our high school football team reached the state championship game, which took place in a neutral location in another city. The team that year, like most years, was majority-Black, with a significant number of White athletes, and a significant number from multiethnic families. A few years ago, a fight on the field at a state championship game that involved an all-white team and a different majority-Black team had led to a drawn-out series of court rulings and sensationalist negative press coverage. When we arrived for the state championship, we found that police officers were stationed at all four corners of the field, holding back enormous K-9 police dogs with chains. The implication was clear: if any of these rough, dangerous, impulsive, inner-city Black boys gets out of line we have no qualms about letting dogs tear their flesh off to keep "our people" safe. Our athletes played the entire game within view of dogs, straining at chains, positioned there to attack them if necessary, because of what local authorities believed about their racial background. It was definitely a "cataclysmic event."

We won the state championship. The local celebrations lasted for weeks. The team had strong Christian student leaders, who used the triumph to highlight the important role that their faith and the faith of their teammates had played in bringing the team together and leading them to victory. Amid the air of celebration, few people had the cultural background to understand what the athletes on the field had felt, or what grandparents who lived through the Civil Rights Movement felt, watching their grandsons forced to live out one of the most triumphant moments of their lives under the imminent threat of police brutality. A few community leaders, however, did their best to explain what the athletes and their families were feeling, and why it mattered so much. Many associated with the football program did their best to listen. "Realization" was taking place.

The next year, our team reached the state championship again, and once again the police dogs were brought to the field. This time, team and community leaders were ready to help frame the experience. Before the game began, the White principal of our school assured the athletes that he was paying attention to the indignity that they faced. The school's Black retired principal spoke next, and at one point, he spoke directly to the White athletes, explaining that to be one team, to choose to understand that walk alongside their Black teammates as the brothers they claimed to be, they would need to accept that other people would begin to treat them as outsiders, too, and disbelieve and deride their experiences. But to be one team meant to stand by their brothers. "Your people become my people" was the message of the day.

We lost the championship game that year, but the coach and key student leaders continued to incorporate the idea of cross-cultural solidarity into the life of the team, bringing realities of inner-city life and cross-cultural collaboration into the team's regular vocabulary. This was "preparation." While the team has not won a championship in the few years since, with the leadership that the athletes found together, the graduation rate at the school soared in the next two years, and the football team took up mentoring roles with younger students on local teams. This "activation" set the team in motion as a force for reconciliation and development.

> Making the turn from a cataclysmic, negative event, to a reconciliation process, to a community development impact, took enormous faith (it wouldn't have happened if most of the key leaders hadn't been Christian) careful listening to leaders of color, and thoughtful leadership from the school, the coaches, the team, and other key influencers. Racial reconciliation is hard work on a long journey, but team sports can become a powerful vehicle for reconciliation if we seize our opportunities and do the work.

But even when the sports world offers us a chance to transform ourselves and our teams through cross-cultural reconciliation, we all still have to face a world whose ruthless power structures reinforce injustice. Serious, long-term, intergenerational leadership is required to translate the personal transformation experienced by athletes on multiethnic teams into changes in the community and the world. A triumphant championship led by Christian leaders on a multiethnic team may change the lives of the athletes forever, but they will still walk off the field into a world where wealth distribution, incarceration rates, and educational attainment reflect a brutal reality of institutionalized racism. Carrying personal and community transformation back into the realities of the world is complex. The kind of interpersonal reconciliation we experience on a sports team is only a step on a long journey toward racial justice, something we will talk more about in Chapter Nine.

The long work of reconciliation, like the long work of community development, requires a faith and persistence that can only come through a connection to God and to His people. While schools, programs, and sports teams can be incredibly important tools for carrying out God's mission, God's primary way of connecting his people on earth outlined in scripture is through the church—something we will explore in the next chapter.

Church: Staying Grounded

To work in Christian Community Development is to put down roots in a neighborhood and persevere through the joys, challenges, triumphs, and pain of a marginalized community for years on end. We will often be misunderstood. Loving our neighbors in our distressed communities means we will face times when the injustices of the world seem crushing and the disappointments seem too much to bear. This work isn't something we can do on our own; we have to stay deeply rooted in a relationship with God, and supported by the community of God's people. And while we can find that community in all kinds of places, including in our sports programs, God's primary directive in scripture for connecting, supporting, and growing his people in order to worship Him and build His kingdom is through the *church*: a body of baptized believers (Matthew 28:16-20) that meets together regularly to encourage one another (Hebrews 10:25), is taught the Word by pastors/elders (1 Timothy 3), serves one another and the Kingdom of God by using their God-given gifts together (Romans 12), guided by the Holy Spirit (John 14:15-31).

The mission of Christ takes place everywhere, but it is fundamentally rooted in the church. All the programs, nonprofits, schools, businesses, and sports teams in the world cannot create a healthy neighborhood if that neighborhood does not have healthy churches, the institution designed by God to grow His people to maturity and mobilize them for mission. The work of Christian Community Development is fundamentally church based.

Sports: An Extension of the Sanctuary

In our work as coaches and mentors, we will encounter many people who use the word "church" to refer to a building, or a Sunday morning "event." While this usage is correct English, the true biblical meaning of the word "church" is as a translation of the Greek word "ekklesia" meaning "gathering." A church is a *gathering of the people of God*. The building that English speakers also refer to as the "church" might really be better termed the *sanctuary*, a safe and holy place set aside for God's people to gather in a special way.

While sports teams can be an excellent mission field, where relationships of trust, brotherhood, and sisterhood act as starting points for sharing the good news of Jesus Christ, for many athletes, sports also function as an *extension of the sanctuary*, a safe and holy place set aside for God's people to gather and work together. Romans 12:1 tells us that one way we worship God is to offer our lives as "living sacrifices," devoting our daily lives to be lived in ways that glorify God. For many athletes, their sports are one of the holiest and most joyful things they do in life, and dedicating themselves to give their all with passion and discipline, to love others as themselves while they do it, and to offer their success to the glory of God, is an act of worship. Their sport is a holy place, where they gather with others to glorify God; an extension of the sanctuary.

Chris Lahr recalls another example from Philadelphia:

> A few years ago, I visited a friend of mine at his new church. He took pride as he showed me the newly constructed building and told me about some of the work they were doing. He showed me a basketball court in their parking lot, and the pavement was faded as it was apparent the court got a lot of use. My friend told me that the court was often filled with neighborhood youth, and that one of the things that led him to this particular church was the presence of these youth—that the "mission field" was right at their door. As we turned to go back inside, my friend informed me that the door we were walking through acted as a "barrier," as the youth rarely came through the door unless they had to go to the bathroom. He longed for them to come in and be a part of their congregation, but there seemed to be little interest. As I looked at my friend, I told him I thought I knew what the problem was... he was looking at the basketball court as the "mission field" instead of viewing it as the sanctuary!
>
> In Philadelphia, we at Timoteo Sports run a flag football ministry for urban youth ages thirteen through eighteen. Of our 250 youth only 32% attend church on a regular basis. Yet something amazing happens each week on our field... youth memorize a Bible verse before being able to play, and after each game the youth stand in a circle as a prayer is lifted up. Our youth are "unchurched" kids, and yet when you ask them what they like about the league they say things like: it's a family, it's a safe place off the streets, it's a place you learn about God, where you learn about the Bible, it's a place I learned to be a leader, it's a place where I was mentored. At Timoteo we are redefining the sanctuary. We definitely believe in the church, and our league currently has twelve churches that partner with us to make Timoteo happen. But we spend more time being the church, being God's gathered people, in real life, than trying to talk our youth into conforming to us in our church settings.
>
> The word "missionary" is actually never used in scripture. But God calls us frequently to be a neighbor! The term "missionary" can

carry a lot of negative connotations in the city, but the word neighbor almost never does, and we are all called to be neighbors. No matter the context (overseas, urban or suburban), a neighbor represents the incarnate Jesus and we are called to show those living in the world a different way.

The football field as a sanctuary is a new concept for some, but for hundreds of youth in Philadelphia, it is making sense. Over the last fifteen years we have seen lives changed and leaders emerge. The four pillars of Timoteo are: Jesus, Excellence, Empowerment, and Partnership. It is ultimately Jesus and his Kingdom values that drive us to produce an excellent product for the youth in our community and call for excellence in our youth. It is Jesus that has modeled for us a way of empowerment through mentoring and discipleship as we partner with people in our community to make a difference. In order to redefine the sanctuary, we must be willing to go where people are at and to live out the Gospel on their turf.

Chris recalls another moment when he became aware about the value of the people of the church being willing to enter into community spaces:

> Several years ago, my wife and I were asked to help chaperone a youth retreat. The highlight of the trip was when my wife and I put on these huge sumo wrestler suits—you should have seen the look in her eyes as she came charging at me with every intention of knocking me down. As she charged at me full-speed I casually stepped to the side and she went zooming by, only to fall on her face. There she was, the love of my life, stuck on the ground in a huge sumo wrestling suit, unable to get up. A true highlight!
>
> This youth retreat had all kinds of activities, a great worship band and, of course, a speaker. The speaker was very charismatic in his approach, and each service would end in an altar call and it was nothing for him to pray for someone or even blow on someone and they would fall to the ground (I am not sure if we had onions for dinner or not). I remember near the end of the retreat, he was giving the final altar call, one of the longest altar calls I had ever been a part of. Initially he asked for anyone who would like to give their lives to Jesus to come forward and several people came. He then extended the call for those who wanted to rededicate their lives to Jesus to come forward. Before you knew it he was calling everyone forward: "If you are wearing a red shirt or white underwear..." Eventually, if for no other reasons than to get the guy to stop, everyone went to the altar except one kid. There he was, a gothic kid sitting in the back row with his arms crossed. The speaker had a field day with him, doing his best to scare the Hell out of him. I can honestly say this was the first time I prayed that someone would not go to an altar to pray. I knew that if he did, it would not have been genuine, and it would have been just to get the preacher to stop.
>
> Eventually the youth got up and walked out of the service. Feeling highly frustrated, I left the altar and went out after him. As he sat outside smoking his cigarette, he started telling me how frustrated he was coming back to this church. He told me that this was not the first time something like this had happened — in fact, he said every time he showed up to this church, they would judge him and made him feel like crap. The young man then informed me that the same church was in the middle of raising funds for a multi-million-dollar project to build a new arcade at the church to reach out to the community. Without my even asking, he shared that there was no way he and his friends would ever enter the likes of that arcade. On the one hand, they would not be able to smoke,

> and on the other hand they would probably have to listen to Michael W. Smith and Amy Grant!
>
> It was in that moment that it dawned on me that the Church is not always called to build their own arcades, but we must be empowered to go into the arcades that already exist! Jesus sent his disciples out into the world—he did not create a mega-building with the hopes that everyone would come to him. In a culture that values sameness and centrality, we want folks to come to us on our terms, we want them to look and act like us no matter what the real state of their heart is. I am not suggesting that youth group kids need to go out into the arcades that exist, and smoke weed for Jesus! On the contrary, I implore the Church to go to the arcades that already exist and live differently. Show the people of the world a new way of living, on their own turf! The same is true in the sports world. Don't expect kids to come into your church to join a basketball league if there are already excellent leagues available through the city. We must be willing to go into the community to serve the community effectively.

Often, the work of Christian Community Development involves bringing holy presence into community's spaces. Sports, which already harness and organized the passions and joys of young people, are an excellent opportunity to expand the sanctuary into the sports world.

Churches and Church Partnerships

This doesn't mean, though, that the traditional sanctuary, where Christians come together to meet on Sunday morning and be equipped for the work of the Kingdom, is unimportant. There is a saying passed around the Fellowship of Christian Athletes: "A Christian without a church is like an athlete without a team." To try to practice Christianity without a congregation, organized in the way the Bible describes, is like a wide receiver running through a crowd of people, hoping someone somewhere will decide to throw him a ball—no matter how good he is at what he does, it is absurd for him to try to do it alone. Christianity is a "team sport"—the Bible says so (1 Corinthians 12).

At minimum, we should be encouraging every Christian athlete in our programs, and every athlete who accepts Christ as Lord and Savior in our programs, to find a local church where they will be loved, discipled, and equipped to serve. Oftentimes, our programs can benefit significantly from formal or informal partnerships with one or more local churches.

Jeff Thompson describes the way that local churches have become connected to the people and programs of 10:12 sports:

> It has been an enlightening experience for our neighborhood teens and adults to see our sports program essentially as an extension of churches in their neighborhoods. In our program the local church has been our primary recruiting ground for finding mentors who are connected with the neighborhood and have a desire to reach our teenage demographic. Generally, those mentors are more influenced by the great commission of Jesus to 'Go and make disciples' then to by the temporary glory of winning sporting matches. Partnering with the church has also served to create spaces where program events such as baptisms, meetings, rallies, practices, games, dinners, trainings, and devotionals can thrive.
>
> Partnering with churches has also given our young men access to individuals and programs offered through the local church, including services ranging from academic help to legal help to job opportunities and training to spiritual growth, along with various other opportunities. Most importantly, partnering with the church provides us a community where our young men can continue to grow when they have graduated from participating in our programs. As we look at the long-term well-being of our young men, we believe that the church community can be their strongest source of support in living the life that God has called them to live.

Other examples might include churches volunteering to feed a local team before games, or to help drive to and from away games. Some churches end up sponsoring teams or even leagues of their own, which may mostly serve members' children, or may serve as an outreach to the community. Sometimes, there is no formal partnership, but church connections help individuals with a calling to work with at-risk young people find the right places to serve. If you are looking for Christian volunteers for a program, local pastors and other church leaders are likely to know who has the heart for the job. Kenny, one of 10:12's coaches, is a great example:

> Kenny came from a rough background. He grew up bouncing around in West Baltimore in some of the most "crime filled" neighborhoods in the area. Neighborhood dynamics had an influence on him as he started selling drugs at an early age. While living this life Kenny was incarcerated and eventually shot and left for dead. One day when he tried to sell drugs to the pastor of a local church, not knowing who he was, the pastor asked to start meeting with him. Before long, Kenny gave his life to the Lord, joined the church and started learning more about what it means to be a disciple of Jesus through a program called One Hope.

He connected with 10:12 Sports, and using sports as a way of serving the church has been impactful for Kenny. Kenny's rough-around-the-edges background was perfect for connecting with local youth who had experienced the streets but were searching for peace. Even to the boys selling on the block, Kenny can be a voice of wisdom, because of his own history, and because of the sports connection. Sports ministry became a bridge between Kenny and the youth—and then between the youth and the church.

Kenny has a unique ability to connect with West Baltimore's young people, and through his church, Kenny has people and resources to support his unique leadership and outreach, as well as a community within which to be refreshed spiritually and emotionally for the difficult mission to which God has called him. Kenny has the experience and calling, the sports ministry is the connection point, and the church makes it sustainable.

Being involved in the league, Kenny is able to use his gifts in a way that serves the neighborhood and serves the church at the same time. His pastor reached him, and in turn, through sports, he is in a position to reach the young people of the neighborhood.

Sports Ministry Broadening the Reach of the Church

We hope that everyone reading this book has found a wonderful, supportive church to be a part of. But we know from experience that some practitioners of Christian Community Development find it difficult to find the right church to embrace their work. Discipling people from the margins of society is central to Jesus' mission, but it can require a special kind of understanding from a congregation.

The good news is, those of us working in community-development-oriented sports ministry have an opportunity to help congregations empower and mobilize a latent potential that already exists in many churches. Usually, plenty of people in the congregation already love and engage with sports regularly, and the potential to mobilize sports as a tool for reaching, discipling, and including people that some congregations might not otherwise know how to integrate into their communal life.

Steve Connor (2002), founding director of Sports Outreach International, introduces his book *Sports Outreach* in this way:

> Let me ask you a question. If a musician, let's say a piano player, walks into your church for the first time; would your minister or the church's leaders know how to best mobilise their skills and talents for the cause of Christ and the health of the church? How about an athlete? If a sportsperson, let's say a football player, walks into your church for the first time; would your minister or church leaders know how to best mobilise *their* skills and talents for the cause of Christ and the health of the church? (pg. 9)

Steve Connor's rhetorical questions illustrate a point: many church members have a passion for sports, but often have no clear way of applying that passion for the cause of Christ and the health of the church. Those of us who coach and mentor in distressed communities know that a passion for sports can be an excellent point of commonality for bridging social differences for the sake of the gospel. By helping people with a passion for sports engage in this way, we help God's churches engage more fully in his mission, empowering both a segment of the existing congregation and a segment of the community to engage in a new way.

New Level Sports Ministries in Battle Creek, Michigan, has an amazing story—a single church seeking to better equip its high schoolers to succeed in employing their God-given talents started a small sports ministry. That ministry has now spawned a three-block complex in the heart of Battle Creek that offers multiple sports as well as arts programs and uses its own programs to teach business and workforce skills to rising community leaders.

Pastor Chris McCoy of Faith Assembly Christian Fellowship, who also directs the ministry, explains how their movement started:

> We started because there was a need for our inner-city athletes to begin to move to postsecondary education, and they were not, because of three areas. First, personal growth—they did not know how to conduct themselves. This could be a result of a lot of things, including their economic situations, but the main thing was fatherless homes. Secondly, education. The school that we were dealing with, education wasn't secondary—it was "third-dary," if that could be a word! The institution that is supposed to be telling

> them that education is the way out of poverty and to success, is telling them that education is not a priority. Then there's the physical piece. They were gifted physically, but because they were lacking in these areas, most of our athletes were not moving to college, to get a free education, to play the sport they love to play. We wanted to help prioritize their lives. It started small, but it quickly grew, to the point that we had to back off, because we didn't have the capacity!

Seeing the complex problem that the community needed to come together to solve, McCoy felt that the only logical answer was to root the solution-building in the church:

> What better place to birth this sports program but out of the church? The Black church is still the strongest institution in the Black community. You've got access to families, access to kids, it's a ready-made volunteer base. You have trust there. And it gives you the ability to move into other areas that are actually going to be the kids' true callings. I play football. I'm a good football player. But my true calling may be that I'm a skilled laborer, I may be a gifted plumber, mason, a skilled businessman, a skilled surgeon.
>
> "The church should take the lead, particularly in the urban community, in addressing our own plight. We have the answer to poverty, to workforce development, to homelessness, to broken families. These are social problems, true, but they are really spiritual problems. That is what God's Kingdom is. The church is the best place for the Kingdom to be most effective, and for God to demonstrate himself in solving problems that the social institutions can't solve. If you look at the spiritual side, we don't fight against flesh and blood, but we are struggling with principalities and those powers of the air. It's not ultimately a fight with people, it's a spiritual battle.

The result of Faith Assembly's sports outreach has been more people in the church and more leaders in the community:

> Now we are breaking down a lot of barriers. It's nontraditional. But it still has all the effectiveness and the power that the traditional church we grew up in still has. It's the tools and the vehicle that's taking the message to the people that could be a little different.
>
> What's happened now is that...you now have a strong spiritual force, black athletes coming into that community. We had a kid that started with us in the ninth grade that is now our attorney. He was made to be a gifted trial lawyer, but we never would have known that if he wasn't in the program. But he's taken New Level

as a pro bono case at his firm in Detroit, they do all our legal work. He did get a football scholarship, but his true gift was something else.

We had a gangbanger—and when I say 'gangbanger' he was a regional director of a gang that went from Michigan to Wisconsin—he had spent time in prison, very well read, I'd been knowing him for a long time. In prison you're reading everything, trying to find truth, trying out different philosophies . . . I knew enough about what he was talking about to gain conversation with him. He was always talking about the community, how he tore the community up and now he wants to give back. He was always asking, "

"Where's the church at?"

So when we opened our sports ministry, we would have eleven hundred people come through. My associate pastor is also a doctor, and we were picking up paper after the game, and when he saw the service of these people, picking up the field, it won him to the church. He still comes, and he's really active in the after-school program, helping others. The Word of God, in sowing an example, in demonstrating who Jesus is, won him. I didn't have to say anything, he just came. That's what happens when you use sports as a ministry.

Our main scripture verse that we use is from Ezekiel 33:33-36, and it describes what's happening:

> Thus saith the Lord God; In the day that I shall have cleansed you from all your iniquities I will also cause you to dwell in the cities, and the wastes shall be builded. And the desolate land shall be tilled, whereas it lay desolate in the sight of all that passed by. And they shall say, "This land that was desolate is become like the garden of Eden; and the waste and desolate and ruined cities are become fenced and are inhabited." Then the heathen that are left round about you shall know that I the Lord build the ruined places, and plant that that was desolate: I the Lord have spoken it, and I will do it.

This is what he's doing right now with the West Side of Battle Creek. It was a desolate land, and those who are passing by are seeing that the Lord is the one who is building these desolate places, And He is going to be glorified. All of that came off of just trying to help high school kids get to college and starting a football program. Because God sees way beyond what we do."

The church is the foundational building block for the gathering of God's people. Healthy neighborhoods need healthy churches, and healthy ministry flows out of healthy relationships between God's people and God's churches. As God's people gather and begin to use their gifts together, God's *shalom* flows naturally from those relationships—which brings us to our next key idea, *redistribution*.

Redistribution: Spreading the Wealth

The work of Christian Community Development begins with *relocation*—becoming rooted in the community. The moral and spiritual foundation of the work comes from *reconciliation*—people being reconciled to God through Jesus Christ, and then being reconciled to one another. One of the goals of Christian Community Development is to produce *redistribution*—a change in the distribution of resources that allows those who were once on the margins of society both to contribute, and to thrive.

When some people hear the word "redistribution," they think of the government redistributing resources through taxes and programs, or charities making donations toward the poor. While either of these can produce real good, these forms of "redistribution" can also produce *dependency*—a situation in which many people have no choice but to continuously depend on either the government or on private charities, rather than be empowered to make their own contribution toward the common good, and receive a just compensation for that contribution. Our ultimate goal is to take redistribution several steps deeper, helping to make sure that the people of the community have both the skills and the opportunity to support themselves and construct their own way forward.

For example, if families in a neighborhood struggle to afford food, a government food stamp program or a privately supported food bank can help alleviate hunger in the short term, which is incredibly important—even one day without food is a crisis for any family. But in the long term, either of these on their own or together lead at best to dependency—with the people of the neighborhood continuing to rely on outside sources for food. If the program ever fails, an immediate crisis ensues. A long-term community development solution might involve a combination of community gardens, a food cooperative, and a locally owned grocery store that each help provide healthy, affordable food, and employs residents, providing income. These interrelated solutions will involve personal development for the residents of the neighborhood that equips them for the tasks and jobs involved — gardening, starting and running a business, etc. And these solutions will likely also involve public structures — land ownership, zoning, business licenses, and more—and may even involve changing those public structures to suit the needs of the community.

Two Sides to Redistribution

Because of this, redistribution as understood by those who practice CCD has two related components: equipping residents to create their own solutions and challenging and changing unjust social structures in order to allow those solutions to happen. As Dr. Perkins is fond of saying: "If you give a man a fish, you feed him for a day. If you teach a man to fish, you may feed him for a lifetime—but we are also going to need to talk about who owns the pond." Knowing how to fish does little good if you don't have access to a place to cast your line.

Those who practice CCD put a lot of energy into education—formal education is one of the main ways we equip young people to succeed, and other forms of community education, from trade and business skills to tax preparation to any number of life skills, equip the people of the community to create their own sustainable success. At the same time, advocating for education equity is essential to these goals; schools in our distressed communities are often underfunded and neglected for social and political reasons for which those in power need to be held accountable. Job skills and readiness are essential for people in distressed communities to become self-sufficient. At the same time, public policies and structures, from the layout of public transportation, to the licensing process for many careers and businesses, to the way that many convicted felons end up excluded from most employment long after they have paid for their crime, need to be changed in order for the people of the community to put those job skills to work. Empowering redistribution that does not create dependency is a two-fold process that involves equipping individuals for success and restructuring communities and their governance to allow that success to happen.

Sports and Redistribution

Our sports programs are uniquely situated within our communities to encourage and empower redistribution. Community sports teams often draw athletes from a variety of economic backgrounds, with their equipment and fees are sponsored by local corporations, allowing all athletes to benefit equally from the skills, mentoring, fitness, and other benefits that the team provides. A local business investing in the opportunities of an economically diverse group of young people this way is a meaningful form of redistribution. While some businesses sponsor teams simply for the name recognition or the tax break, a community-development-minded program might invite a sponsoring business to interact with the athletes in a way that broadens their horizons or deepens their skill set, such as touring the business, shadowing an employee, learning about the industry, or even offering an internship to one of the athletes. If used well, these relationships between athletic programs and corporate sponsors can become important sources of connections for later in life.

Many of our community sports teams are directly tied to public schools, and funded by public money, offered free or at no cost to any student who can make the team. Not only does this offer recreation and other benefits of athletic participation to community members, but teams often serve as support networks and safe spaces for students who are otherwise marginalized within the school system. A community-development-minded coach at a public school can use his position to support his athletes' education and development, both by lending or finding academic or social support to the athletes themselves, and by advocating for them within the system as a whole. Many coaches at public schools have stories of being a confidant to an athlete in a time of crisis, intervening in the life of an athlete who was headed off track, or helping create a way forward for an athlete who was in danger of being discarded by the educational system. By serving as a part of these athlete's support network, these coaches are engaging in a form of redistribution, supporting the educational attainment of marginalized students on their way to success.

In turn, many, many young people from distressed communities are able to secure funding for their college education through athletics. While the promise of a "scholarship" is often misunderstood by well-meaning young people and sometimes exploited by those who make false promises (we will talk more about this in Chapter Nine), the fact remains that athletic scholarships have funded the educations of thousands of young people from poor communities for decades, serving as another, important form of redistribution for our young people.

In many communities, school and community athletic programs are a place where young people from the community can connect with trusted mentors who impart knowledge, skills, and values, and serve as an important context for developing the leadership and supporting the futures of young people. Many community-based sports programs will tailor their strategies and programming to instill important values in their athletes. Some will do this without advertising it; others will make it an expressed part of their goals.

To better understand how our sports programs offer us opportunities to redistribute opportunity and resources within our community. It helps to understand the *multiplex* nature of our community development efforts, something that has helped shape Chris Lahr's work with Timoteo in Philadelphia:

When one thinks of mentoring, it is easy to think of the one-on-one Big Brother/Big Sister model that has long been successful for many people. Though one-on-one relationships are important, Timoteo has discovered the importance and power of group (team) mentoring, which we call "multiplex mentoring." Anthropologist Max Gluckman (1955) coined the helpful terms *multiplex* and *simplex communities*. In our daily lives, we all have roles that we play. My (Chris's) life roles include husband, dad, friend, co-worker, general manager, youth worker, web-guy, son, brother, uncle, nephew, grandson, fantasy football guru, mentor, offensive coordinator, and coach, and I am sure there are others.

In a simplex community, the people we interact with through our different roles do not connect. For example, the people I go to church with have nothing to do with the people I work with, coach with, or live with, etc. In a simplex community we have single-role relationships, and our lives become fragmented. When we only connect with people in one facet of life, it is really easy to act one way at church, and another way on the field, sometimes called "bracketed morality"—because the people in our lives are disconnected. Those wanting to see what Dr. King called "beloved community" and true justice will continue to wait, as very little of this can be accomplished in a simplex society. In the simplex mode, we are often limited to denominationalism, mentoring ineffectiveness and surface level friendships.

All youth are high-risk and in great need, but those living in oppressed communities have even greater needs, as they have greater hurdles to face, including poverty, violence, poor educational systems, racial biases, and often, single-parent families. In most cases, a mentor coming from another community for an hour a week is simply not enough. Youth in urban communities need more than a mentor, they need a mentoring community, a mentoring multiplex.

A multiplex community occurs when two or more individuals within my network of human interaction are linked to each other through more than one role--the people I go to church with I also work with, spend holidays with, clobber in fantasy football, mentor with, and so on. In a multiplex community we become more aware of a person as we connect with them in various roles. Multiplex communities have strong social ties and create an environment in which it is easier to learn, and to live out justice. I would argue that multiplex communities are "beloved communities," in the sense that interactions become broader than our personal denominations or homogenous groupings. In multiplex communities we realize our giftings as well as our inadequacies and need for others.

Multiplex mentoring involves a group of people doing the mentoring. Instead of a single mentor (coach) expected to be the guru in the relationship, the mentor is only a piece of a larger group of people pouring into our Timoteo youth. Multiplex mentoring is holistic mentoring: our goals go beyond our kids getting better grades and good jobs; we want our players to live to their fullest capabilities, raise healthy families, overcome anger issues, and other markers of wholistic wellness.

We are made for community. There is too much emphasis in our society on being "independent;" multiplex mentoring calls for interdependence. We are called to use our gifts to their fullest, to embrace our weaknesses, and rely on other people who are strong in our weaknesses.

Multiplex Mentoring and the Power of Community

Several years ago my wife, Lara, and I were going to school in Wilmore, Kentucky. During this time we discovered this concept of multiplex communities and started to be intentional about building relationships that were multiplex in nature. One aspect of our multiplex community took place while doing a Bible study at a Salvation Army homeless shelter for women and children. One night as we were getting ready to start, a woman (Sophia) walked in and asked if this was the Bible study. We assured her it was, and she informed us: "I will come in on one condition—no one touches me! I know how you Christians are, always hugging and whatnot!" Thinking she may have been in need of a "chill pill," we eased her mind that there would not be a hug-fest after Bible study. She went on to tell us that she was agoraphobic, meaning she had a medical condition causing her to have an absolute fear of people! I guess it wouldn't be so bad to be agoraphobic if you were rich—you could get an X-Box, lock yourself in a room and game away. But being agoraphobic and homeless and reliant on others is a very difficult set of conditions.

Throughout the Bible study Sophia relaxed a bit and seemed to enjoy herself as she laughed at my corny jokes and enjoyed talking to my wife. As the Bible study wrapped up and everyone filed out, Sophia stuck around and told us her story of homelessness and the difficulties she had on the streets while having a mortal fear of people. After a lengthy talk I asked Sophia if I could give her a "verbal hug" to close out our evening. Without hesitation she told us that she felt as if God had reached down to her and told her that it was ok, and she gave my wife and I physical hugs that night!

Now, in a simplex-style community we would leave the story at that, and we may even label it "successful ministry." But the reality of the situation was that Sophia needed much more than a hug; she needed beloved community. For the next several weeks we got to know Sophia better and continued to laugh, hug and build trust. Eventually we invited her to attend a house church nearby, called Communality, that had recently started up and that Lara and I had been attending. I'll never forget the first time we took Sophia to church as she huddled in the corner of the porch in fear, while we gingerly introduced our friends to her. She enjoyed it, but she was still overcome by fear. Each week we continued to visit her at the shelter, and she went with us to church, slowly but surely building up confidence.

Around Thanksgiving we decided to hold a love feast for our friends. As I gazed around our dining room table, I saw an interesting gathering of folks that included seminary and college students, folks who were homeless and formerly homeless, people who were elderly and those who were young, and folks from various racial backgrounds. I initially wondered what we would talk about, but then it happened—the conversations started flying, the laughter filled the air and the power of hospitality was manifested. Hospitality is a lost art in our society (Pohl, 1999). If recovered, can be a great tool for building a multiplex community. Around the dinner table relationships were strengthened and Sophia received from the "formerly homeless folks" a lead for housing! Within a few months of all of this, Sophia had a place to live and was completely healed of her agoraphobia—so much so that she became the mama for the little house church we initially took her to, and if you tried to sneak past her without getting a hug you could get in trouble!

Sophia continued to grow closer to Jesus in the context of her new multiplex community. She developed relationships with people in her apartment complex as well as with people in the church. Through the church she stayed connected with other homeless folks and was able to assist them along their journeys. An amazing thing occurred as we built our beloved multiplex community—Sophia did not become too dependent on our relationship with her! Though we stayed close, she also built healthy relationships with others within our multiplex. Before you knew it, she built her own multiplex community! In a simplex relationship, folks can get burned out if "the helpee" is completely dependent on "the helper." A multiplex community allows many folks to be involved in the work.

The same holds true for mentoring your team in an urban context. The coach should not expect to have all the answers, but the coach should seek key relationships with people that can assist in giving holistic mentoring care to our youth, drawing on the young person's own network of support as well as those in the community. Within Timoteo we have identified four faces of mentoring that are a part of our multiplex mentoring approach.

Mentor as Coach

In his book *InsideOut Coaching: How Sports Can Transform Lives,* former Syracuse University All-American and NFL star Joe Ehrmann (2011) describes his journey from a young athlete using sports to escape a stress-filled childhood, to a coach and mentor using sports to transform communities. Joe's "Inside-Out" coaching philosophy informs us of two different styles of coaching: transactional and transformational. A transactional coach is all about the win, and he will use the players to lift his own self esteem. In transactional coaching, competition is most important, and mentoring is not a main goal. On the other hand, transformational use their platform to mentor youth and help them become well-rounded adults. Transformational coaches not only spend time working on the x's and o's of their team, but the "Y's" as well. They ask themselves Y (why) they coach and create an environment where their players can ask the "whys" of life.

The mentor coach is a key person in terms of building a relationship with the player and acclimating them to the team and the overall culture of Timoteo. The mentor coach is often in a position to help players through life decisions, leadership development, family situations, and character building, and the mentor coach often acts as a father figure. On the field they provide discipline and a positive authority figure that is genuinely interested in the youth. The mentor coach is also very human and can model an appropriate way of dealing with anger, as it isn't uncommon for the best of coaches to be overcome by anger in competitive situations. But a transformational coach is not afraid to apologize, or to address the team when they fall short. Mentor coaching is not about being perfect, but about rebounding from our imperfections. In our sports programs the coach is often the most important connector between the young people and other caring adults in the community.

Mentor as Teacher

Timoteo did a survey of their players and discovered that 92% of them had a desire to go to college. That same group was also asked how many complete their homework on time, and only 44% said they did. We are told in the Bible that "where there is no vision, the people perish" (Proverbs 29:18, KJV). We have discovered that even with a vision, our dreams perish if we are not taking the appropriate actions to make those dreams become a reality. Just because you have a vision to go to college, doesn't mean you will actually go to college—and I can guarantee it won't become be a reality if you are unable to finish homework on a regular basis.

One of Timoteo's core principles is excellence. The mentor coach can call for and often obtain excellence from their players on the field.

The next step is to show they can also obtain excellence in the classroom. One simple method to start a youth towards academic excellence is through asking them about their grades, and better yet, checking the grades yourself. In Chapter Six and Chapter Seven we will learn more about Emerald Youth Sports and Memphis Athletic Ministries, two CCD sports programs that have found important ways to bring athletics and after-school academic support together, contributing in key ways to the redistribution of resources and opportunity through educational support.

One benefit of a multiplex approach is that you can have educators who love youth, but do not necessarily like sports, actively involved in your sports program as a teacher, and not a coach, and coaches who support the work of the teachers at the school. In the past, Timoteo developed a program called the Locker Room, and one aspect of the program was bringing in an educator to help youth fill out their FAFSA's and write their college essays. Because the training was sanctioned by Timoteo, the players knew they could trust the Locker Room, and even though we held the Locker Room at a local college, they ended up feeling right at home.

Mentor as Boss

Another very important face of multiplex mentoring for our youth is the mentor as boss. Nearly every kid we questioned in Timoteo either has a job or wants one. When asked why kids don't have jobs, answers ranged from not knowing where to look to feeling intimidated by asking for a job or interviewing, so at the Locker Room, we also trained youth how to interview effectively, and how to fill out applications and resumes, contributing to community redistribution by getting them ready for their first paying jobs.

We have also created job opportunities within the Timoteo program itself. Each spring football season we keep our eyes open for youth ages 16-18 that are leaders in the community to work as summer camp coaches for youth ages 10-15, and each year at summer camp 150 young people are led by their peers, who receive leadership training and run their own teams. Youth are employed through the summer camp and the expectations are high. Though we show a lot of grace, as a mentor-boss we also reprimand our youth and at times fine them for lateness or disruptive behavior. Just as we have seen these younger leaders excel as players on our fields, we now give them a chance to succeed as peer leaders to younger youth on those same fields, mentoring them in the skills they need to succeed in the workplace. Just as we practice transformational coaching, we also aim for "transformational bossing." We find that as we hold high expectations, we are rarely disappointed, and when we are, we are able to work with the youth to rebound and excel.

Mentor as Pastor

Wholistic mentoring involves connecting to the youth in every facet of their existence, including their spirituality. Timoteo has a tradition of the "game day verse:" in order to play, you have to recite a verse that reflects the theme of the season. We also have inspirational quotes as an alternative for those of other faiths (or no faith) who do not want to quote the Bible. We were surprised at how many of the youth mentioned the game day verse as one of their favorite parts of Timoteo--for some, it is the only Bible teaching they receive, and they appreciate the positive messages given to them in a context they can understand.

Even so, coaches got wrapped up in the game and often missed going over the verses with the youth, so we started asking that each Timoteo team have a "chaplain," a pastoral figure to work with the team. We discovered that having mentors as pastors (chaplains) has been an effective tool for connecting with the youth at a deeper level, and in some cases they have been a bridge between our players and the church. As pastors and other church people have connected with teams, more people from churches have come out to the games. The youth take notice when people from those congregations go crazy on the sidelines for young people they barely know – when the church people show up on Saturdays, some of the youth end up showing up on Sundays.

Effective community redistribution of resources and opportunity happens in the context of a strong and healthy network of relationships. Research from the Fuller Youth Institute (Powell, Griffin, & Crawford, 2011, 79) suggests that across the socioeconomic spectrum, each student needs an average of five adult mentors during their teen years in order to develop a healthy adult faith life. Relationships that support young people in their growth and development, impart key life and workplace skills, and create connections for future success have the long-term result of setting up the youth of the community for interdependent success.

A Caution: Rejecting the Savior Complex

Embracing a multiplex understanding of community distribution of resources means rejecting a common and tempting trope that is often projected on our work as Christian community developers—the *hero complex* or *savior complex*. The savior complex promotes a narrative of a talented, generous, and educated person coming to the rescue of a community and its young people in dire need.

While we may love semi-true classic sports movies where a bossy-but-loving suburban mom takes in a homeless boy and lovingly bosses him all the way to the NFL, or a no-nonsense alumnus of a failing high school comes back as a coach to whip hapless boys into shape, holding their athletic dreams hostage until they come to appreciate his iron-fisted discipline, these hero-based narratives can be extremely harmful to true community development, which depends on the collaboration and empowerment of the community as a whole.

Many of the young people we work with will show real gratitude in tangible ways, and there is nothing wrong with this. Others with a survival mentality will heap praise on adults as a survival tactic, to continue receiving whatever they believe the adult can give, which requires wisdom to handle. Some leaders and media outlets will praise a "community savior" because it is easier than facing the complexity of the real problems at hand. But as good as it feels to be somebody's hero, and as much praise as we might receive from others, we need to be ready to push back against this tendency, and lift up the contributions of all those within the community who do the difficult daily work of restoration and development, and the many people who pour into the lives of the young people of the community together.

It is especially important that we recognize our duty to respect the sacred role of the families of the young people we serve. The nuclear and extended family is the essential God-given structure for the formation of young children, and it is part of the role of every adult in their lives to help them carry out the fourth of the ten commandments: *honor your father and your mother* (Exodus 20:12a). In our distressed communities families are often degraded as dysfunctional or culturally deprived, undermining the role of the most important adults in our young people's lives. Some of our young people will be raised in two-parent, nuclear families, and others will be in nontraditional arrangements with single parents, aunts, uncles, grandparents, or other caretakers. No matter the arrangement, we are there to *serve* young people and their families, respecting their values and offering ourselves and our sports programs as part of a community support network as they raise and support their children. (In rare cases we will need to be the ones to protect young people from truly abusive situations, which requires an expertise beyond the scope of this book).

Most importantly, the Bible is clear, there is only one Savior: "For there is one God and one mediator between God and mankind, the man Christ Jesus, who gave himself as a ransom for all people. This has now been witnessed to at the proper time" (1 Timothy 2:5-6). When people praise us, that is our chance to glorify God for working through us and acknowledge the many people He has brought together to lift the community up.

A Second Caution: Fundraising

While the long-term goal of Christian Community Development is to create an environment that redistributes access to resources and opportunity, fundraising—a more direct form of redistribution—will likely be a part of many of our programs. Fundraising can be an excellent way to give people the opportunity to contribute to and support good work that they would not be able to accomplish on their own. Giving is both a spiritual discipline (See 2 Corinthians 9) and a spiritual gift (see Romans 12) that brings the Body of Christ together for the common causes of God's Kingdom, and our fundraising efforts are an opportunity to help this take place. Still, we feel the need to suggest caution around areas where fundraising can cause significant problems in Christian Community Development.

Contributing to the restoration and development of our distressed communities requires a commitment to a philosophy of redistribution and empowerment. Often, people or institutions will offer significant funding to initiatives in distressed communities, but that funding comes with "baggage:" expectations, based in a certain worldview, about how those initiatives will be run. Some of those expectations may be based in narratives that are harmful to the community. When those expectations are challenged, the funding is used to try to control or manipulate the program or ministry. Some people who raise funds for work in distressed communities end up facing the choice between staying quiet about their communities' deepest justice issues and receiving more funding, or speaking up, and losing support. In other words, a lot of money comes with strings attached.

Despite these potential pitfalls, partnerships across the resource scale can be very successful. Fundraising for initiatives in our distressed communities is about cultivating *partnerships*—relationships with people and institutions committed to seeing the community thrive and building the relationships necessary to see that happen. When this takes place, it is another beautiful picture of the *shalom* of God's Kingdom, as the Lord draws together unlikely people for heavenly purposes, and the world witnesses the generosity, partnership, and transformation that characterize God's people. There is great beauty and purpose in the way God upends the pattern of the world, *redistributing* resources by drawing together and *reconciling* his people across social class as a daily reality in our programs, ministries, and communities. A multi-economic partnership in mission is a non-negotiable part of God's calling for His church. 2 Corinthians 8:12-15 says, also quoting Exodus:

> For if the willingness is there, the gift is acceptable according to what one has, not according to what one does not have. Our desire is not that other might be relieved while you are hard pressed, but that there might be equality. At the present time your plenty will

> supply what they need, so that in turn their plenty will supply what you need. The goal is equality, as it is written: "The one who gathered much did not have too much, and the one who gathered little did not have too little.

Redistribution is an essential goal of Christian Community Development. A major source of distress and dispossession in our communities is the unfair distribution of opportunity and resources, and development can only take place when this distribution is made more just and more fair. Redistribution can begin with fairly simple rearrangements of wealth and opportunity, but in the end, it takes a long-term focus on opening doors, equipping and supporting people, and altering social structures so that the community achieves healthy interdependence and sustains its own growth. The challenges that our communities face in achieving this are often so complex, they cannot be addressed as separate issues; community development requires what Dr. Perkins calls a *wholistic* approach.

Wholistic Sports: Heart, Soul, Mind, Strength

In 2018 Freddy Amil, a Timoteo alum, graduated from Arcadia college. Freddy is from Philly and did not live too far from the Timoteo field where the flag football league ran every spring. Freddy started showing up at Timoteo games when he was about thirteen years old. He talks about his humble beginnings, and how he lived in a one room apartment with his parents who struggled with drug addiction. Life was hard for Freddy, as he had to grind through poverty on a daily basis, and often went to school hungry if he happened to go to school at all.

Freddy credits Timoteo as being the one thing he needed to turn his life around during his last year of high school—only what he found at Timoteo wasn't just "one thing." He mentions the importance of the game day jobs that Timoteo offered during the season as key in sustaining him on a weekly basis. Timoteo started offering game day jobs for youth during the season, ranging from keeping stats to cleaning and setting up the field to filming the games, as an effective way to teach new skills, and to offer financial assistance for those struggling to pay the league fee. As it turns out, some of the kids actually rely on the game day job to sustain them and help them eat.

Freddy missed a lot of school his first three years of high school. He says that as he became a part of the Timoteo community, he began to have pride in himself as he excelled on the field, giving him the confidence that doing well in school was something he could accomplish as well. He came to excel in school as well: he was on the honor roll his senior year and the only day of class he missed was an excused absence to go visit Arcadia University, the school he would eventually graduate from! It was also through Timoteo that Freddy started attending church and built a relationship with God. He says game days were transformative for him, as the team started looking to him on a weekly basis to lead them in the game-time prayer; Knowing the guys were looking to him to do this increased his faith.

Freddy's story is one of many that point to the importance of a wholistic approach to doing sports ministry in an urban context. Through Timoteo's coaches, he learned the game of football and was able to succeed on the field. But through the game, Freddy developed a close-knit family that helped support him through his formative years and gave him the courage to graduate from college. Freddy grew physically, emotionally, spiritually, academically, and even vocationally because of the wholistic care he received starting at the age of thirteen. Wholistic care is complex and takes time, as changes start as small seeds. But with time, maturity and great care, the seeds blossom into something spectacular.

The Wholistic Approach

Our distressed communities face a complex and interrelated set of issues: historic factors such as deindustrialization, institutionalized racism, and economic exploitation have set the stage for a social crisis; a lack of local resources leads to underfunded schools and infrastructure, which in turn contributes to poor physical and emotional health for many residents. Key services and business that might help are often hard to access. Our point is not to paint a dire picture of our communities, but to point out that the challenges we are motivated to overcome as we develop the community from within are complex and connected to one another. A piecemeal approach to individual "issues" is not enough; Christian Community Development requires what Dr. Perkins describes as a *Wholistic* approach — the spelling is intentional — an approach that sees the physical, social, mental, and spiritual needs of people and communities as interrelated parts of a whole.

For historical and philosophical reasons, many churches have come to see their role as addressing the "spiritual" needs of people, leaving physical, mental, social and emotional needs to other institutions in society, except perhaps as a "hook" for an evangelistic program. Some of us have heard criticisms that we, or our churches, should "stick to the gospel," "leave politics alone," or "stop mixing faith with social issues." These comments stem from a specific history of division in the North American church, but they do not reflect Jesus' true intentions for his people.

As James wrote (2:14-17), ""What good is it, my brothers and sisters, if someone claims to have faith but has no deeds? Can such faith save them? Suppose a brother or a sister is without clothes and daily food. If one of you says to them, "Go in peace; keep warm and well fed," but does nothing about their physical needs, what good is it? In the same way, faith by itself, if it is not accompanied by action, is dead." Jesus calls us to love our neighbors with a concern for their whole being.

This is captured well in what Jesus called the "Greatest Commandments:" "Love the Lord your God with all your heart and with all your soul and with all your strength and with all your mind" and "Love your neighbor as yourself" (Luke 10:27). We are called to put our whole selves to work for the sake of God's love: our emotions (heart), our intellectual capacities (mind), our bodies (strength), and the deepest spiritual core of our very selves (soul). In turn we have the same love for our neighbors as we have for ourselves, working to ensure that they can use their full capabilities for God's purposes. This includes making sure that our neighbors' needs—physical, emotional, spiritual, and mental—are met, so that together our community can reach its full potential to serve the Lord by serving one another.

We learn what those needs are by *listening to the community*—again, we may believe we have a sense of what the community needs, but the people as a whole, living out their lives on a day-to-day basis, will have the best collective sense of the needs that need to be met in order for the community to move forward. Coach Gordon likes to tell a story of wanting to build a fitness center, but realizing the immediate need was for access to a washing machine and dryer—the community needed a way to clean their clothes before they could focus on larger issues of overall health (Gordon & Perkins, 2013, 103-104). Meeting wholistic community needs requires us to listen carefully before tackling interrelated issues.

Sports and Wholistic Development: Heart, Mind, Soul, Strength

Sports are an excellent venue for the wholistic development of young people. Many athletes instinctively know that what they do somehow engages their whole being, and science backs it up—for many North American youth, sports are one of the only places where they engage their "whole self" at once. That means that those of us who coach and mentor young athletes have the amazing privilege of helping them discover, develop, and integrate their full selves. Participation in sports is widely touted by senators, CEOs, and stay-at-home-parents as a key part of their character formation. Of course, this does not happen automatically; programs need to be run and structured properly to take full advantage of this experience in order to take advantage of the profound mental, emotional, and social elements of team sports.

Dr. Jeff Duke of the University of Central Florida has blended years of research into a philosophy he calls "3 Dimensional Coaching," which incorporates the wholistic nature of the experience of young athletes by recognizing that the athletic experience incorporates what Duke calls the first (physical), second (mental/emotional), and third (spiritual) dimensions. Much of coaching takes place in the first dimension, where the physical aspects of the sport are learned. Much of athletic performance and the associated life skills learning, however, takes place in the second, psychological/emotional dimension, where issues like motivation, confidence, emotional regulation, and team cohesion create the essence of the team sport experience. But real internal transformation takes place in the wholistic spiritual dimension, which unites the physical and mental/emotional experiences, giving them meaning through identity, character, and purpose (Duke & Bonham, 2013, 69-75). The passion that many of our young people have for sports is rooted in the third dimension: they find success, meaning, acceptance, and joy in the context of the game. The most successful coaching *and* the most successful personal transformation recognizes the importance of the third dimension—the spiritual realm of identity and significance. Lasting change of the kind we seek to make through sports-based Christian Community Development must be rooted in meaning and purpose, which can only happen through a *wholistic* approach to sports of the kind Duke describes.

The science of youth development increasingly backs up the idea that exercise and sports are not just an "extracurricular" portion of a well-rounded lifestyle, but an interrelated component of wholistic development. While many education systems in North America emphasize visual and verbal learning through lecture, repetition, and writing (which are very important), Dr. John Ratey has spent a career documenting the connection between physical activity and learning. He points to an experiment at a suburban high school, where adding an early morning gym class for struggling students propelled the school's test scores to some of the highest in the nation (Ratey, 2008, 12-15). A similar experiment in low-income neighborhoods produced similar results (32). Recent neurological and educational science suggests that our sports programs are offering far more than recreation; participation in sports can add life-altering learning capacity for students who struggle in school and deal with toxic levels of stress. It is no surprise that our marginalized young people gravitate to athletic fields—their experience there is reprogramming their mental state in a way they can't label but know instinctively that they need to be whole.

And while physical activity by itself does little to develop character per se, the character-enhancing experience that so many people have playing team sports shows the profoundly *social* element that ties together the team sport experience. This will not happen automatically, but by using the social aspect of team sports to reinforce a positive value system. Joe Ehrmann, whose *InsideOut* coaching philosophy Chris brought up in the last chapter, describes how coaches can draw out the social lessons of athletics by fostering *liberty* from the negative self-concepts that are forced on so many of our young people, *respect* for self and others, and *moral courage* to face the pressures of life, which requires a relational intentionality beyond the "transactional coaching" required to win games in the short term (Ehrmann, 2011, 140-155). The social role of athletics within society, as well as it's team nature, makes sports a teaching ground for justice issues as well (162-70). The brain activity ignited by physical activity, combined with the social nature of team sports and games, makes our sports programs an incredibly fruitful environment for instilling and reinforcing the very values that make Christian Community Development possible.

These intellectual, emotional, social, and spiritual benefits of sports will only be realized if we are intentional about how we coach and mentor. Simply throwing a ball into a field and letting kids loose does not build character or produce transformation; at best, it will simply *reveal* the character already present in the young people. Only a consistent set of values can pull together and make sense of a wholistic approach to coaching and mentoring young people. The philosophy of Christian Community Development presented and applied in this book represents such a value scheme, and those who practice CCD are convinced that each community must practice careful listening and leadership development to flesh out its own set of values.

Meeting Wholistic Needs

Our sports programs have the potential to provide an excellent wholistic development avenue for our young people. But a wholistic approach also needs to recognize that our young people likely have components of their wholistic wellness that are going unmet *outside* the context of our programs. As we saw with Freddy's story, their development on the field and their development within the community are inextricably linked.

As those of us who coach or mentor in our distressed communities know all too well, we will work on a regular basis with athletes who at times feel physically unsafe because of abuse or the threat of violence in the neighborhood, who may not always know what they will eat or where they will sleep, or who may lack access to healthcare, basic education, or the finances, transportation or support necessary to access these things. These needs concern us deeply, and many of us have lain awake at night, concerned over young people whom we know are heading home to unsafe situations, or answered a shy and reluctant phone call from one of our athletes, asking us to help her procure groceries, shoes, a jacket, or perhaps even money to pay a family bill.

These experiences make us wonder what we could possibly do to help, individually or systemically, in the short-term or the long-term—and these needs also impact the effectiveness and feasibility of our sports programs themselves. Athletes who show up hungry, can't show up at all, or show up bringing the baggage of basic insecurities will engage very differently with the youth development components of our programs. Our ultimate goal—the interdependent thriving of the people in our community—cannot be reached if these needs are not met.

In the mid-20th century, Psychologist Abraham Maslow developed what he called the *hierarchy of needs*—the basic needs the people have that build on one another until a person is able to operate as their full self. Simply to stay alive, people must first have physiological needs met (such as food and shelter), and then must be physically safe. People then need love and belonging to develop properly, at which point they can achieve self-esteem, and finally what Maslow called "self-actualization," which we would argue includes not just the self, but a high level of healthy interdependence with others.

Some of our athletes in distressed communities are not having the needs near the bottom of the hierarchy met, making it difficult for more internal forms of development to take place. A basketball and a Bible verse can do a lot of good, but a basketball and a Bible verse won't put food on the table or stop a bullet – not directly, anyway. Our sports programs can help develop a wholistic future for our young people by helping to meet these needs—sometimes within the program itself, sometimes through the relationships developed through sports, and ultimately by empowering our young people to meet their own needs.

Physiological and Security Needs

When young people go hungry, are unsure where they will stay, lack basic health care, or live lives where they fear for their safety, the entire trajectory of their development is affected in ways that an astute coach or mentor will notice. Oftentimes, those of us committed to community development are able to find ways to meet some of these needs through our sports programs.

In one program we know of, a longstanding partnership between a church and a local high school football team began when the coach asked the church for something incredibly simple — food on Thursday nights. It wasn't that hard to get people to bring food on game day, especially because this meant free admission to the game. But many of the athletes were not eating dinner on Thursdays, affecting their ability to play (as well as their long-term development). The church agreed to bring food on Thursdays, and a partnership developed that evolved into meeting many other kinds of developmental needs.

In addition to meeting needs programmatically, it is often the relationships formed through community sports programs that help meet the wholistic needs of our young athletes. Most of us who coach or mentor in our distressed communities have stories of buying groceries or clothes or connecting a young person with a job, simply because the team sport experience brought people close enough to understand and meet one another's needs. When done in an empowering way, without a savior complex, these connections help bring the community together in the way that God intended when he commanded us, "Love your neighbor as yourself."

Belonging and Esteem

Once basic physiological and security needs are met, people are free to search for *belonging*. One of the reasons youth sports programs have such a powerful impact on people's lives is the sense of belonging they create. Seemingly superficial things like uniform colors and team names reinforce a sense of togetherness. The intensity of the shared experience of victory and defeat gives young people a sense of acceptance that is reinforced by the emotional thrill of the action. Many young people in distressed communities have experienced an intense sense of social rejection. Rejection may stem from experiences of poverty and the social stigma that often comes with experiences as an ethnic minority in a structurally racist society, or from any number of factors associated with social marginalization. When we work to make our sports programs inclusive places that capitalize on the sense of belonging that team sports create, these efforts can go a long way toward meeting the basic need for a sense of belonging. As Christians, we know that the Bible teaches us that our ultimate sense of belonging is found as children of God, reinstated into God's family through faith in Christ (Ephesians 2:19-22). As Christian coaches and mentors, we can build a culture in our sports programs that show the same sense of welcome and belonging to our athletes that Christ has extended to us.

In turn, there is another reason that so many young athletes develop important parts of their core identity through their sports experience: Maslow finds that a sense of belonging lays the groundwork for the development of *competency* and *self-esteem*. As we saw in Freddy's story at the beginning of the chapter, when Freddy developed competence and was affirmed within the context of the game, it told him something not just about football, but something about *himself* – who he was and what he was capable of – ultimately giving him the confidence to apply the same effort to his schoolwork. The sense of competence that young people develop first by *playing* translates easily into the rest of their lives; what begins as *play* soon bolsters a sense of capability and identity that allows them to navigate new and more high-stakes challenges.

For programs that include travel, either to other cities or to places of importance within our own communities, this travel can serve both to broaden horizons and worldview, and to reinforce the young people's own identity and understanding of community in the context of a wider world. Many a young athlete has seen the great sights of North America after being eliminated early from AAU tournaments in famous cities (Welp, that's it kids, nice work, you win some, you lose some...who wants to get a cheesesteak and see the Liberty Bell)? We can be intentional about our travel, choosing sites and experience that enrich the ability of our young people to build self-knowledge and cross-cultural competency.

Partnerships and Wholistic Rootedness

There are many ways in which our programs, and the personal relationships our programs build, can meet the wholistic needs of our young people. But the challenges and strengths of our communities are both complex, and it will often be better to turn to a partnership within the community to meet those needs, and in doing so, support other leadership within the community, rather than duplicate what is already being done by adding it to our own program. Camp Clutch found this to be true as they looked for ways to sustain connection with their athletes throughout the school year:

An effective program is capable of realizing their strengths and weaknesses. There's absolutely nothing wrong with acknowledging that there are areas where your organization's programming cannot meet the particular needs of your clients. Realizing our inability to meet the needs of all students through our summer basketball program, Camp Clutch sought additional means to engage and nurture our youth throughout the duration of the school year. One of the ways we did this was through offering one-to-one mentorships for youth and families that requested additional support. Fully aware that our coaches were incapable of meeting those needs for various reasons, we (with the help of a community organization called L.I.T. City) sought to recruit individuals in the community who could commit for two years to spending time with a mentee once a week, for a minimum duration of two hours per week. The L.I.T. City program conducted all screenings and training. Virtually all mentors were not coaches within the program. Instead, they were individuals who desired to work with youth, but did not feel equipped to coach kids. However, by providing this opportunity, desirous individuals were able to engage in youth ministry. This component, while often overlooked, allowed Camp Clutch to reach new levels of youth engagement. It is through acknowledging our weaknesses that we gain strength. Our weakness was made stronger through the support of those mentors.

In Philadelphia, Timoteo Football has developed a creative connection with Eastern University that has borne fruit for the youth of Timoteo and for the college:

Providing wholistic care through multiplex mentoring can be accomplished in creative ways. Not many of our youth in Philly have ever gone to a college for a campus visit that was not located immediately in Philly. To be honest, if I were ever to pass around a sign-up sheet to go visit a college in some far-off place, not many of our youth would jump at the opportunity.

We discovered, though, that those same kids were highly interested in joining us for a "training camp" that would take place at this same far-off campus (Eastern University) and would include a scrimmage with college kids. Suddenly the sign-up sheet was filled, and kids were already talking trash about how they are going to show the college students how to play flag football. We also informed the youth that not only were we going to run drills and a practice on the college's turf field and scrimmage some college kids, but we were going to get an exclusive tour of the campus followed by all the free food they could eat in the cafeteria!

We didn't have a single objection to the trip and—lo and behold—they loved every minute of it. We started the day running a very difficult practice so they would get a lot of their energy out. After practicing for a couple hours, we went on a tour of the campus. We were amazed at how into the tour the youth were, whether they were planning on going to college or not. Long story short, we had three of our players decide to attend Eastern University...they all got in...they all got scholarships...and they all graduated!

Creative partnerships are important for offering wholistic care to young people. Sports ministry can provide a creative outlet for developing vital partnerships that can assist youth with their futures. Sometimes thinking outside the box and packaging services to youth in a language that they can understand, and embrace will be much more effective.

When community development works the way it should, our programs are one component in a larger network of solutions, and our relationships are linked in with a network of relationships that together lift the community toward self-sufficiency.

Dr. Scott Brooks (2008), director of the Global Sport Institute at Arizona State University, describes in the book *Against the Wall: Poor, Young, Black, and Male* how in inner-city Philadelphia, basketball serves as an organizing point to counteract the social disorganization of inner-city neighborhoods:

> In this context, basketball is a critically important activity. The sport is organized in many different ways that bring adults and youth together, and serious participation and integration into basketball activities build and bridge networks, providing additional resources and opportunities for young men. Young men are encouraged to maintain or regain positive sense of self through being given an opportunity to show that they can succeed at something positive and should not be presumed criminal, guilty, and inherently bad...basketball is not simply a 'hoop dream'—young men's unrealistic hope and fixation on basketball and other athletic endeavors as a ticket out of the ghetto. Rather, basketball is an institution and way of life that enables young men to cope in the current context and reduces the social-psychological impact of being negatively stereotyped and marginalized." (pg. 148)

In this environment, basketball serves to teach life skills and frame identity: "Playing ball seriously requires goal setting, discipline, and commitment and often leads to higher self-esteem and increasing social pressure to live up to idealized expectations" (150). But perhaps more importantly, basketball broadens young men's social support system, introducing them to mentors and others who can help them navigate young adult life.

Brooks recounts the true story of a young man who, after the loss of a loved one, engaged in a physical fight at school which landed him in serious trouble with authorities who viewed him primarily through a lens which labeled him delinquent, culturally deprived, and in need of control and punishment—an all too frequent occurrence for young men in distressed urban neighborhoods. While the brutality of the legal process threatened to derail the young man's entire future, "[his] connection with the adult men in the basketball league meant that his story differs from other young black men in trouble with the formal authorities" (156). Through the basketball league, he had connections to retired criminal justice workers as well as an active probation officer who walked him through the legal process; one of his coaches was able to arrange for his community service to be carried out with the basketball league itself. The social support network developed through the league served to ameliorate the effects of negative stereotypes and the brutality of the criminal justice system.

As Brooks' research suggests, the use of sports to strengthen social organization and connections is especially important in our distressed communities. Sports bring together people who might not otherwise encounter one another and add additional mentors in the lives of young people, strengthening the community as a whole and improving outcomes for the most vulnerable.

Trauma-Informed Coaching

While our programs and the relationships and partnerships they foster can work wonders in terms of meeting the wholistic physical and developmental needs, we also need to be cognizant of the specific effects that having those needs unmet has on young people, an area of science that has grown by leaps and bounds in the past decade, and to be cognizant of the incredibly unique role that sports can place in reversing those effects.

When children have their needs for basic physical or security needs unmet—experiences like missing a meal, being physically attacked by peers or adults, watching a caretaker or other trusted person hurt, or not being sure where she will sleep—they form pathways in the part of the brain (called the amygdala) that processes threats. This then alters their behavior going forward. Reminders of these experiences, which can be very difficult for others to recognize, can "trigger" that person into a "fight, flight or freeze" response that mimics a life-threatening situation. Much of the difficult-to-manage behavior of young people from difficult backgrounds stems from these experiences, and a young person who has many of these experiences, especially if they are unprocessed, can begin to exhibit emotions like anger and mistrust almost like personal traits rather than states of being. The awareness and treatment of this phenomenon has come to be known as *trauma-informed care,* and its practice in the sports world as *trauma-informed coaching.*

When adults combine an understanding of this process of behavior pathway formation with knowledge about how physical activity positively impacts both learning and stress management, the results can be enormously positive. Andy Neilsen is a national trainer with trauma-informed coaching leader Up2Us Sports which, through a partnership with AmeriCorps, places, trains, and supports over 350 coaches across the country annually. He explains that when coaching emphasizes the elements of sport that intervene on the effects of trauma, it can create an environment where young people feel safe and can begin to heal and thrive in their participation. "Trauma is fundamentally an experience of losing control. Activities like playing catch, dribbling a ball, or even jumping rope can provide a predictable rhythm shown to calm a mind experiencing the toxic stress of trauma," Neilsen says. Physical activity also opens pathways in the hippocampus, the part of the brain responsible for learning. "Sports programs that understand trauma and the brain science behind it can return some control to their athletes by giving them the opportunity to practice managing the feelings associated with stress through competition. Coaches can connect a supportive team environment to a protective layer of peer and adult support that allows players to gain confidence and ultimately thrive in that competitive environment rather than being overwhelmed by it." The skills players learn and develop to handle the stress of competition can also transfer to skills that help them manage stress in school, home, and work environments in the future.

Neilsen has coached in a number of contexts, from community-based programs on Chicago's South Side and West Side to internationally competitive youth teams. The great news, he says, is that trauma-informed coaching mirrors great coaching at any level. "Great coaching begins with a strong relationship between coach and player. The relationship serves both as the foundation for trust and growth that is at the heart of sports, as well as the beginning point for understanding what the player needs. From the young person who is consistently triggered by a loud sound to a high level player wanting to overcome a skill plateau, a relationship with a coach is necessary to identify and support the growth in skill that is at the heart of positive experiences with sports."

For coaches who see difficult behavior, Neilsen suggests two fundamental frameworks that Up2Us Sports teaches to support coaches and players in these situations. First, behavior, no matter how challenging it can be to a coach or disruptive to a team, is almost always the result of experiences that young people have had, and not a deliberate attempt to ruin practice or a game. "At Up2Us Sports, we say that 'behavior tells the story.' And with this understanding, it's less important that we as coaches know exactly what that story is but acknowledge that there is one and that their behavior is in some way a response to whatever may be going on. Often, players just showing up on a given day is them doing the very best that they can." When we see behavior as telling a story about a potentially traumatic situation, we see that building a deeper relationship based on empathy for the story provides the best path to mitigating the behavior.

The second strategy reframes behavior of all kinds as a skill-building opportunity. "If a player comes late to practice, coaches can write them off as not committed," Neilsen offers. "But if a player misses a free throw, we teach them and support their growth as a shooter. Why can't we look at showing up on time as a skill that needs to be developed?" When coaches look at behavior through a skill framework, they not only avoid the frustration that often attends difficult behavior, but they also start to develop strategies to improve the behavior with the athlete. What follows is a reinforced belief in the growth mindset—the idea that we can all become better versions of ourselves—in both coaches and players for sport and non-sport contexts.

For decades, young people from difficult backgrounds have insisted that their sports participation, especially in contact-heavy and fast-paced sports, has "helped them with their anger," "taught them how to overcome adversity," or "taught them to control their feelings." In the past decade, we have come to understand that these statements are rooted in complex brain science, and even more deeply true than most young people are aware. Our sports programs in our distressed communities are oftentimes *the* best venue for this healing to take place. Given the destructive behaviors that result from unhealed childhood trauma, the healing process that is taking place in our sports programs is literally saving lives.

To fully support this opportunity, coaches need to be aware of strategies for engaging, redirecting, and ultimately healing trauma-based behaviors that most people find difficult to manage and even more difficult to understand.

Changing the Culture: Embracing Balance

While sports teams often contribute much needed components of physical activity and social development to the wholistic development of young people, we also see many young athletes embrace sports as an obsession, to the exclusion of other important activities and identities in their lives.

The Emerald Youth Foundation in Knoxville, Tennessee, is striving to help the young people of Knoxville strike an important balance in their lives. Emerald is a CCD-based ministry that was born out of a single youth group twenty-seven years ago, and now operates in nineteen neighborhood locations across the city of Knoxville, focusing on the wholistic development of children and youth, or, as Kevin Dubose, one of Emerald's area directors, calls it, "comprehensive engagement."

Emerald values reconciliation, the healing of the community's long-term hurts; their newest and largest facility is under construction in Knoxville's Lonsdale neighborhood, along a road that has historically divided the black and white parts of the city, and is now home to a growing Latinx population. This move is intentional.

"Community is a big part of it," says Kevin, "Our multi-million dollar complex is literally next door to the housing development, in a neighborhood where the high school built for the neighborhood is vacant since 1989, where there is gun violence—we are building a connection point where parents can come and build a sense of belonging, a sense of pride. I don't underestimate that. I think that if you want to win [the neighborhood], you have to win the pride. Individually, you are building skill, but in the community, sports are a connection point for relationships to happen, for mentors to happen, for great things to happen."

Emerald is a citywide operation, with departments to handle fundraising, marketing, program development, human resources, and, increasingly, information technology, as every location needs its own set of computers. But the focus stays on the wholistic development of Knoxville's young people.

"We work hard on culture, we have a pretty long hiring process . . . we do that somewhat intentionally too, so that people understand who we are and what we are doing, and really prayerfully consider joining and what our culture is," says Chief Operating Officer Shara Shoup. "Research from the Search Institute basically says that there are a certain number of assets kids need to have in their lives in order to succeed, and we've grouped those assets into three categories: faith, learning, and health. The scale we want to get to is 200 promising godly leaders every year that are meeting those outcomes. All the scaling [growth] is to produce those outcomes."

Emerald's Director of Sports and FCA Urban Reach is a "remainer" named Sanford Miller—a lifelong Knoxvillian whose journey took him from being an athlete in Emerald's programs, to college football at the University of Tennessee, to a career in banking, to his current position at Emerald ("didn't 'make it out' at all!" he quips). Sanford is now focused on giving back to the city that raised him through wholistic athletic ministry to children and youth:

> I went to the University of Tennessee. Playing college football in my own hometown was a humbling experience, because everyone that followed your high school career was waiting for you to be

that breakout player. But once you get to that level and learn the business of it, and you don't have the success you always wanted, it humbles you real quick. But I'm a better man from it, and those opportunities have opened doors for me, so I'm very grateful.

A guy who played football with me said, 'I'm leaving Knoxville, Knoxville hasn't done anything for me.' And I said, have you ever asked, what could you do for Knoxville? 'Cause I guarantee if you decide to do something for Knoxville, it's gonna come back to you. This guy was a captain at the University of Tennessee! And he said this city's done nothing for him. It cheered for you to get you in the NFL, buddy—that's for sure!

I came to Emerald in 2006 as an Americorps and was promoted to sports coordinator. I worked about two years and then took a job in banking and spent two years as a branch manager in two local banks here. I came back to Emerald about two years ago in advancement and fundraising, and then went back to sports coordinator. Now I'm over about 1500 athletes, 180 teams, and ten different sports. It's wild. To God be the Glory.

Having grown up an athlete in inner-city Knoxville, Sanford draws on his own experiences to create a wholistic approach for the 1500 athletes in Emerald Youth Sports:

> I know what sports did for me—sports changed my life. It gave me an opportunity. As a ten-year-old kid, coach said to me: 'One day, son, you're going to play college football.' Really? I never thought that would be possible. So then, that's all I heard. You're going to play college football one day. So, when it came time to graduate, I took the ACT eight times. My focus was on playing college football, but no one ever said anything about Sanford Miller going to school to get a degree! So all those different experiences that I went through—flunking out of college, getting back into college, and people giving me more opportunities, it was like, when I have the opportunity to correct that for someone else, I'm going to be able to use all those different experiences to speak right into it, because I was there. A lot of those things that these kids are going through, where there's a parent in prison, things like that, I've lived it.

As the sports coordinator at Emerald, Sanford has focused on building a culture that reflects a wholistic approach to youth development, moving away from the singularly sports-obsessed youth culture to emphasize education, faith, and health in the context of athletics:

> We are really trying to change the culture of what inner city sports look like. Just growing up from playing EMC sports, I've seen a shift toward 'it's all about sports.' There's no balance, there's more practice time, practice time, practice time, camps, tournaments, camps, tournaments—and there's no balance of lifestyle for kids. So, what we are doing with this sports philosophy is creating a balance, making sure we have adequate amount of faith time, family time, schoolwork time, practice time, game time, and social time, just with kids being kids. I tell all my parents and coaches, think about those six different things, that's a lot to ask of a kid, just to find that balance.
>
> All they have ever known is "it's all about sports"— "Coach, I need more practice time," "Coach, I need more performance training time," and we say, "Well, we're more about your body being healthy, not overworking your muscles" — that's wholistic approach. It's been a challenge, it's gonna take a while to get everyone on board...slowly walking with kids and showing them that this is a lifestyle that we are trying to create, not just a particular season. If we are doing tournaments, we do them every other weekend. We probably won't travel anywhere more than three to four hours away, and we protect Sundays and Wednesdays. A lot of them are like, "Can we go here? Can we go there?" and I say, "No, spend time with your family!"

> One day, we had FCA devotion going on, sixty kids there, and the leader says, "Would anyone like to read scripture?" A hand goes up, and everyone laughs cause this kid raised his hand. And the guy said, "What are you guys laughing at? This is your next leader right here." He was bold enough to be nine years old and say, "I want to read scripture in front of everybody." That's the life skill part of it—I'm willing to stand up and read and lead, in front of a room of sixty people, boys and girls—and we saw parents coming in sticking their head in saying, "That's my son!" The dad was pulling his phone out, like, "I didn't know my son had this in him." We are building confidence in kids. This is not just a Sunday or Wednesday thing I'm doing; I can lead, and use my faith, in sports, in performance training. Its huge in development, just giving kids the self-worth in knowing that it's bigger than just sports.

Sanford has helped Emerald build a culture that brings faith, education, and health together into a wholistic lifestyle where faith is more than Sundays and Wednesdays, physical health is more than a sports season, and education and family life take priority. This happens partly through solid relationships with local schools:

> We can help kids out with ACT/SAT Prep, college visits. Our college and career ministry is top-notch. It's almost like a guidance counselor away from school, who pretty much walks with you on your college or career or finding your true calling. We have life coaches, to walk them through the day to day—if you're going home and you're not used to having food, so you've got to either do homework or go find something to eat—what that looks like. Some of them are going home trying to take care of little brothers and sisters, so how do you balance doing your homework and their homework?

Emerald has taken the vision of a single urban youth group and grown it into a citywide program that is bringing neighborhoods together, meeting wholistic developmental needs for youth and families, and partnering with local institutions. The programs and partnerships in every community will look different. Our sports programs are some of the best environments available in our distressed communities for meeting wholistic needs, supporting wholistic heart-mind-soul-strength development, building community, identity, and self-esteem, and healing the effects of the trauma of those needs going unmet.

Success in the wholistic development of young people paves the way for another important part of Christian Community Development: *Empowerment.*

Empowerment: Lifting Each Other Up

If the foundation of the philosophy of Christian Community Development is the three R's: *Relocation, Reconciliation,* and *Redistribution, Empowerment* is the thread that runs through the whole philosophy, holding it all together. Empowerment, or cultivating power in others, is the end goal of redistribution, reaching a point where a community can provide for its own needs.

While the distribution of worldly power is an important concern in restoring and developing distressed communities, Christians know that true *power* comes from the Holy Spirit, and the rearrangement of worldly powers without the awakening of the Holy Spirit will do little to bring about the justice, peace, and wholeness that God intends for His people. The Bible teaches that each person is made uniquely in the image of God (Genesis 1:26-28), and that each person is also gifted by the Holy Spirit (Romans 12). The *empowerment* that those who practice CCD speak about, then, is about the Holy Spirit awakening each person's gifts, and those gifts being recognized, affirmed, and included by the community itself and the wider world. For too many reasons, this is not happening in our distressed communities, because worldly structures do not allow that potential to be used, because stereotypes and prejudice distort that image of God in the view of others, or because people themselves have internalized negative ideas about themselves. Empowerment means recognizing and including the *dignity* in each person in the community.

In turn, recognizing, affirming, empowering, and advocating for the dignity in each person lays a foundation for the social and economic empowerment that is a major goal of community development. The most important solutions for the community lie primarily within the people of the community itself. As these gifts are drawn out, gifts that will include things like leadership, entrepreneurship, advocacy, stewardship, and other gifts that build the peace of the community as a whole, the community will better be able to self-organize for the social and economic transformation that is necessary for the community to thrive. *Empowerment* means helping this to happen.

We need to be careful about attempting to make people in our own image instead of the image of God. Oftentimes leaders, whether native to the community or from outside, are eager to teach people how to do what they themselves have done. The results are far more impactful, however, when we recognize that the unique image of God in others will be different from ours. Sometimes this shift requires significant cross-cultural and mentoring skills. As we discussed in Chapter Five, there is a good deal of charity and even "development" work that can create *dependency* instead of empowerment. Sometimes, we will know a way to get something done quickly or effectively, but it will be better for the long-term empowerment of the community to make room for others to do it in their own way.

Empowerment, as understood by those who practice CCD, has a glorious cycle to it. Leaders are first empowered by the community as they engage in the listening and reconciliation necessary to take up leadership. In turn, those leaders empower others within the community to take action and leadership of their own. This glorious cycle lifts up the community's ability to imagine and create its own future, by affirming the dignity and including the contributions of the community as a whole, even those the world may be prone to dismiss or leave out.

Dignity Through Sports

The wholistic nature of the athletic experience affords us a unique chance to recognize and empower the dignity of those in our community. At 10:12 Sports in Baltimore, weekend football games have brought a joy and sacredness into community spaces in a way that few other events do:

> 10:12's Saturday games have become an event that the community respects as something positive. Drug dealers move their whole operation when they know we are going to be there. When our guys are out there, there's a sense of pride, ownership, and joy for the whole community, even people coming outside on a Saturday, residents that are consumers of the drug activity, end up stopping there and finding an unexpected joy. It has transformed the field as a community space, almost anyone will stop by and cheer these kids on. Guys passing by walk up and down the sidelines, encouraging the boys. Parents and friends stop by to cheer, and soon they are cheering for everyone's children, getting to know people they didn't know before. In that sense, the kids are part of the community and have something to offer, they're giving everyone a way to come together. They're bearers of good news, without vocalizing it, they're displaying it, inviting people in—these are our kids, this is our safe space, this is our community, our community's future. It's a picture of God's shalom, a moment of peace and joy, even in the midst of some tough circumstances.

Sports have a way of *gathering* people – not just the people on the teams, but the friends, family, fans, and supporters who are drawn to the game – and this gathering can build power and peace in our communities. In some of our neighborhoods, whether because of community dynamics or the negative stereotypes of authorities and outsiders who see gatherings of young people as potential disturbances, sports may be one of the *only* environments in which this can safely bring dozens of young people together in one place foster joy, channel excitement, and develop leadership.

Strength-Based Thinking

One way to affirm the dignity in our athletes is a way of thinking about the development of young people known as *strength-based thinking* or *strength-based discipline*, which is a personal form of the *asset-based thinking* we discussed in Chapter Two. Dr. Scott Larson and Dr. Larry Brendtro (2006) apply strength-based thinking to work with high-risk teens in chapter four of their book, *The Resilience Revolution: Discovering Strengths in Challenging Kids.*

As we discussed before, *deficit-based thinking* describes a problem in terms of what is missing, and a solution in terms of how to provide that missing thing—often from an external source. This is often applied to the development of young people: when a young person is unable to meet a standard or goal that has been set for them, they are considered to have a *deficit* in that area. Many professional psychological and developmental diagnoses are framed in terms of deficits. The solution is typically presented in terms of a strategy, or sometimes a medication, that will help "cure" that deficit. A student who cannot sit still in class may be diagnosed with an attention deficit; a student who struggles with her math homework may be considered to have a learning deficit in the area of mathematics. However, important questions go unanswered: who set these goals, and do they match the gifting of the young person in question? Or do they match the needs of a certain institution or program, without much concern for the young person himself?

Strength-based thinking, on the other hand, asks questions like, "How can this young person use the strengths that she has to meet the challenges in front of her?" and, "Based on this young person's strengths, what are good goals to set for him?" It is possible that the young person who has trouble sitting still needs more active time during the day, or that the young person struggling with math in a class where most information is delivered orally is a visual learner. The goal of sitting still may have less to do with the young person's overall health than with a school's desire to operate in a certain way. When young people fail to meet standards, strength-based discipline asks, "How could this problematic behavior be a *strength gone wrong?* The girl who always questions the adults may have a strong sense of justice, but need help applying it. The boy who always fights may be protective of his friends but need to channel that impulse better. The girl who takes apart everything she finds may have the thinking patterns of an engineer. Behind problematic behavior is often a strength, or as the Bible says, a gift, a piece of the image of God in that young person—but he needs to learn to use that strength in the right way. Punishment does little to change this behavior, since it is so close to the young persons' nature, but redirecting the strength can work wonders.

We use strength-based thinking in our sports programs all the time. Young people often choose their sport based on their gifting and body type, and coaches choose athlete's positions and roles based on the best use of their strength. While many failing systems in our distressed communities are treating our young people as though they have deficits in need of "fixing" and overusing punishment to the point of crippling their lives, in our sports programs they find that their strengths are tapped to make contributions to the whole, and the gifts that are at the core of who God made them to be are used as assets. Our young people may be more comfortable playing their favorite sport than in other circumstances, making their gifts easier to identify and develop. We have found it often to be the case that a coach may know more about a young person's positive qualities than anyone in her life, besides usually her parents. If we are aware of this, our sports programs can become places where young people's gifts are discovered, affirmed, and brought out.

Jeff Thompson has found a way to use sports as an entry point for deeper kinds of affirmation:

> Sports are a chance to give compliments and recognize strengths that would not otherwise be received. Kids want to hear they are good at sports, and we use that as a chance to draw out of them

what is there. Because the sports identity is valued, we can call out the image of God.

In our program culture, we started out by calling out superficial aspects about being good at the sport, but we gradually moved to naming aspects of how they see manhood being called out in one another, how they see servant leadership in one another. Guys really enjoy being encouraged about athletic stuff, but to move on to aspects of character, you have to break down the walls. They aren't just going to come out and say, "You're a compassionate individual, you show empathy well." Starting with encouragement about athletics is a way to get the wall down, to get to that point, to process what it means to be a man of integrity. And then we are able to affirm them in that.

That way, it's within reach. It's not intimidating. Public acknowledgment of athletic ability, guys will readily do that. When that becomes part of the culture, we can ask them to think deeper, we can draw on the teamwork aspect of sports, the character aspect of sports, to get down further in somebody's heart, somebody's soul, to move to something guys can carry into every aspect of their life.

One story in particular reminded Jeff to look for the wisdom God has already placed in our young people:

> Tyrone, a kid I was mentoring, got into a situation where guys were on his front stoop, and they had a little problem with his cousin. They went inside the house, and all of a sudden, the guys started shooting through the window into the house. His family hit the floor and immediately he called me. I asked how he was doing and he said "I'm not doing well at all. Guys are shooting through my window into my house."
>
> As a mentor, I thought I needed to come up with some solution as to how to handle this. I was trying to tell him how to process this and work through it, and he stopped me mid-sentence and said, "I just called you because I wanted to pray."
>
> I was short-sighted in how I was going to handle that situation. In my mind I did not immediately bring Christ into that crucial time, but in his mind, it was like – "Coach Jeff you talk so much about Christ being who I should go to. I'm trying to take you up on what you always say." That's where I should have gone. But it took me being taught by him to realize he had what he needed in him. I just needed to be there for him.
>
> The Bible says we have treasures in jars of clay—there is a lot of wisdom in our young people, if we look for it and call it out. I've learned to be in a place where I'm constantly learning from the young men at 10:12.

Sports as Emotional Training Ground

For many young people, sports programs are an emotional training ground. When handled in the right way, team sports are a way for young people to experience peak emotions, discover new states of mind, make mistakes in a low-stakes environment, and train themselves to handle their emotional ups and downs. And for many of our young people, gaining control over their emotional responses leads to control over their destinies.

In many distressed communities, a cultural gap between students and their middle-class teachers creates significant difficulties in successfully engaging and educating students, contributing to the "school-to-prison pipeline" phenomenon we discussed in Chapter Three. Jamie Jessup describes how Camp Clutch tailored its programming to help empower young people in Winston-Salem to gain the emotional control to navigate difficult situations with authority figures, empowering them to take hold of their own futures:

> One of the most significant impediments to the success of our children in the classroom is their inability to express their thoughts and emotions adequately. On far too many occasions, as a classroom teacher, I have witnessed a student go from zero to 100 on the anger scale in a matter of seconds. Whether it is due to an injustice or a simple misunderstanding, a student's inability to control his or her emotional impulses results in demonstrative, boisterous, and sometimes physical response which ends in time out of the classroom via ISS, OSS, or expulsion. As we know, the more time out of the school, the higher the likelihood of a student to drop out, a higher risk of criminal activity, which could result in a higher probability of incarceration (also known as the classroom to prison pipeline).
>
> It could be argued, and I would likely agree, that the majority of punishments rendered on children of color rarely match the level of the infraction. It is no secret that students of color are disproportionately penalized in comparison to their white counterparts. Additionally, the teacher workforce is a disproportionately white female population in comparison to all other subgroups in education. Consequently, cultural dissonance will set in, resulting in excessive punishments for minor infractions, for children of color. It appears apparent our school systems must consider culturally relevant and sensitive training for our teachers to avoid unnecessary misunderstandings. The reality that systems will prioritize the proposed training is quite a ways from actually happening due to limited budgets and awareness. Therefore, it is imperative our children learn to navigate a system where they will be misunderstood if they don't learn to play the communication game.
>
> Those who follow, watch, or play sports understand the necessity of effective communication. Coaches communicate with players, and players talk with one another. Referees communicate with each other as well as the coaches and players in the game. If at any point in time there is a breakdown in communication, the game plan is likely to fail. Through observation of players in games and practices at Camp Clutch, it became clear to us that effective communication with each other was going to present significant challenges. Players would argue over seemingly trivial matters and break into near fist fights to defend their belief. Needless to say, these actions prevent the team or player from being successful.

Before camp, our coaches participate in cultural bias training, which allows them to explore their own biases about students from under-resourced communities and situations we serve. Many times, the assumptions we carry about a particular group of people influence how we speak to them. For example, educational studies have shown that we tend to approach Black and Brown boys and girls as young people who lack parental guidance, and consequently, need more love. The forms of love we tend to serve are either a laissez-faire passive love or a fierce/tough love approach. Therefore, we only speak to them in ways that either enable or degrade them. Unfortunately, this produces an adverse effect. It is essential we find ways to talk to students that communicate, "I come from a different space, but I seek to understand how I can speak with you in a manner that challenges you but affirms your dignity."

Throughout Camp Clutch programming, players participate in character education courses (also called life coaching) where they learn leadership skills, which include the ability to listen and speak, resolve conflicts, and solve problems. Players are encouraged to practice those skills and strategies in the classroom. After leaving the class, the students are encouraged to practice these skills on the court. By learning these skills, students are better able to advocate for themselves once they leave our program. This is not to say that every student conducted themselves the way we wanted them to when challenges arose, but we saw efforts from each student to make a change. An effort to make a change is better than no change at all.

Jamie's experiences are supported by years of research by Dr. Howard Stevenson, Professor of Urban Education and Africana studies at the University of Pennsylvania. In his book *Playing With Anger: Teaching Coping Skills to African American Boys through Athletics and Culture*, Stevenson (2003) and his colleagues analyze how they use a method called PLAAY (Preventing Long-term Anger and Aggression in Youth) to build emotional empowerment for handling the "culturally relevant anger" (21) experienced by African American boys.

This form of mentoring involves "affection," or connecting emotionally with young people as they play the game, "correction," or confronting and reframing anger when it emerges, and "protection," helping young people discover the self-knowledge to handle difficult emotions (140-143). Mentors "intervene during the moments of tension for boys as they engage in a sport that raises their level of imagination and motivation to points at which personality strengths and challenges are revealed" (147). Stevenson's research explores in detail the emotional dynamics of athletic participation for inner-city boys, and the potential for mentors to frame this experience in an emotionally empowering way.

As Stevenson (2003) notes, "Play is considered to be the one time children receive therapy without therapists" (48). Clinical psychologists do not need to be present for playing, including playing sports, to be a therapeutic and emotionally empowering experience for our young people. As we consider the role of sports in their lives, it is important to realize how often they are using their experiences in the sports world to build the kind of emotional regulation and resilience they will need to dissipate anger, overcome challenges, and live healthy adult lives--and to realize that when they trust us to coach and mentor them, they are trusting us to participate in that process.

Ultimately, it is safe, restorative relationships that make emotional development possible. Consider the story of Dave Garcia:

> Dave grew up in the Kensington neighborhood of Philadelphia, sometimes referred to as the "Badlands" for its violence, and the drug epidemic that runs wild on the streets. When Dave was in elementary school, he often spent time playing football in the neighborhood with his friends. In 2010, one of Dave's friends invited him to play in the Timoteo flag football league. Initially he was hesitant to join a flag football league because he liked to hit people--but when he heard they were handing out free cleats he quickly got on board. Dave would go on to play in Timoteo from 2010-2014 and he was the all-time reception leader when he "retired." Dave would not only go on to make the Timoteo Hall of Fame, but he became a coach and mentor to his community.

> The streets of Kensington have enough drama to make anyone angry, and Dave had his share of anger inside. It was important that the Timoteo field was located in the neighborhood that Dave lived in. Not only was he able to easily access the field, but he was shown a model of a new way of life in the very neighborhood that caused him so much anger. Although anger would rear its ugly head from time-to-time on the field, the culture of Timoteo was different, more peaceful, and coaches and fellow players would often jump in to make sure the anger did not escalate into a full-fledged brawl.

Dave says that it was the mentoring of other coaches that helped him overcome his own issue with anger. When he got angry, instead of kicking him out of the league, his coaches would be patient, offer grace, and challenge him with a new way of dealing with that anger. A few years after his playing days were over, Dave became the head coach of a Timoteo team. Dave would go on to win his first championship as a coach, but he says that was not his best season, because once again anger reared its ugly head. Timoteo holds coaches to a higher standard, and uncontrolled anger does not have a place on the sideline while mentoring youth. Instead of suspending Dave, the Timoteo staff took Dave out for wings and discussed his anger and the options for him going forward as a coach. Dave said it was at that meeting that things turned around for him, as the staff offered to pay for counseling to address some of the deep-seated issues causing the outbursts of rage. The following season, Dave's team did not return to the championship--but he said it was his finest coaching yet, as he was able to control his anger and focus on the important aspects of coaching, such as mentoring his players and walking with them through difficulties they face on a daily basis.

For Dave, Timoteo was not simply a sporting event that occured at a random field in his neighborhood. Timoteo was something he took home with him through life lessons and deep friendships created on the field. Timoteo has become a family to Dave. With family there is good and bad that often come wrapped up together, but in the end, family works together to make the community around them a better place for all.

Social and Economic Empowerment

As the God-given gifts inside the people of the neighborhood are brought to life and empowered, the stage is set for the social and economic empowerment of the community, a component of the redistribution we talked about in Chapter Five. For this to take place, people also need to be equipped with the tools and skills to put their gifts to work, which means investing in things like education, job skills, and social capital. For sports programs connected to schools, a healthy working relationship between coaches, administrators, and teachers helps this to happen. Many nonprofit sports programs have found effective ways to incorporate these kinds of experiences into the program as well.

Memphis Athletic Ministries, as we discussed briefly in Chapter One, is a CCD-based sports ministry that serves children and youth in seven locations across Memphis, Tennessee. MAM has operated since 1998, and according to its mission statement, "exists to coach, grow, and lead the youth of Memphis by helping them discover their identity in Christ and their purpose in the community."

The most impressive of MAM's locations is their Grizzlies Center, built in partnership with the NBA's Memphis Grizzlies. Coach Changa Cooper, a Florida native and Neighborhood Director for the Grizzlies Center, reinforces the importance of engaging the community culture in order to cultivate "remainers" and "returners:"

> Our primary deal is, we want to hit the culture, we want to collide with it, hit it head on. Whatever the culture is bringing, we engage it, we talk about it, we build off it, we want to use it as a steppingstone. We're not afraid of what the kids deal with in school. They've got questions, we try to give them as many answers as we can centered around the gospel...The end goal is to hopefully inspire kids to one day come back and give back to their community.

Local and national partnerships are central to MAM's work. MAM works closely with local schools, tracking students' attendance, grades, and behavior in comparison to their peer group on a daily basis, allowing teachers, parents, and MAM coaches to collaborate on creating a healthy way forward for their students. MAM also partners with the Up2Us Sports Network and the Junior NBA.

While it is in the nature of some sports programs to focus mostly or entirely on either young men or young women, gender equity and access are ongoing issues in the sports world, and MAM's mission is to welcome any young people in Memphis. Randy Odom, MAM's CEO, says: "People ask, 'what's the demographic you're trying to reach?' I say, 'the kid who walks through that door.' Achieving a gender balance required some intentionality: "We let the ladies come in [to a room] and said, 'Make it your space.' We used to be probably 70-30 guy-girl, but when we started hiring young ladies, putting at least two of them in the gym, and then creating a space like this, our attendance is almost 50-50."

MAM is focused on empowering the young people of Memphis, and it was through listening to the community that Memphis Athletic Ministries came to focus on certain key needs. Important among these is literacy, which builds a foundation to focus on areas of long-term empowerment, as Coach Cooper explains:

> The reason we got into literacy is that, in Memphis 73% of the kids are below reading level—all county, not just urban, but suburban. So, we partner with Literacy Mid-South. They train all of our staff, our teachers, they give us an Americorps Vista who is full-time, and so we are able to make sure every elementary kid goes through that piece.

> In middle school, our focus is social-emotional skill development, homework help...[the athlete's] team will have study hall and coaching through sports. In high school, it's more of [finding] a clear career path – "Are you going to go to college? Are you not?" – the mentoring piece, and discipleship runs through the whole gamut. And so in high school it's more about using the influence of the coach, the team, to find a clear career path. How do we help you get job ready? Career ready? Each age group has a different focus, but they all fit together.

The result is a wholistic form of empowerment that draws together education, life skills, career readiness, and discipleship. MAM Coach Maria Garcia has seen the direct connection between literacy education and community empowerment: "When a child learns to read English, it empowers them to defeat what society thinks of minorities – especially first-generation Latin Americans like myself." MAM Coach Mariah Moore shares the value of the strength-based approach she uses, empowering kids for their future by identifying the strengths that will bring them through struggles: "I teach because I want kids to know that they can do anything they put their minds to. I don't do it for money or praise, but because children are our future. I want to help push them to be the best versions of themselves! Figuring out what motivates them and learning their struggle and strong points inspires me to find a way to deliver a fun-filled learning experience. Every day is different, and there's never a dull moment!"

Community empowerment is about drawing out and investing in the gifts that are already present in the members of the community, and then making sure that the community is equipped with the tools, skills, and access to spaces and services to put those gifts to work, overcoming obstacles, creating solutions, and building the well-being of the community as a whole.

Empowering Stories

Another way we can use our sports programs to empower our communities is by telling stories in an empowering way. From time to time, members of the media and community stakeholders will be eager to hear dramatic stories from about violence, dysfunction, and desperate young people meeting middle-class Christian saviors. But when we are asked to tell stories about our communities, we have a chance to tell those stories in a way that glorifies God by revealing the dignity and resiliency of His image inside our neighbors. The Bible tells us (1 Thessalonians 5:11) to "encourage one another and build each other up." When we tell stories about God's work in our community, we have a chance to build up and encourage our neighbors by the empowering way we tell our stories. When we talk about what we do in our sports programs in private and in public, we have a chance to paint a picture of loving, energetic, and resilient young people, a picture that counteracts stereotypes of violence and dysfunction and lifts up the image of God in our neighbors.

Jeff Biddle recalls times when he realized the importance of telling stories in an empowering way:

> One year during spring break, we had an event at a local park with a group of kids. The local news showed up to interview me (he only talked to me—not any of the kids) and he kept asking questions implying that if not for this event, all these kids would be out on the street "getting into trouble." Now, constructive activities for kids are important, but it just wasn't true that these kids would have been "getting into trouble"—these were some of our core leader kids, spending the day building fellowship and celebrating. I kept trying to tell that story, but this reporter was bound and determined to take home a story about all these dangerous troublemakers being corralled there at the park by a local hero (me) so the rest of the city could live in peace, while the cameraman zoomed in on the faces of these (mostly Black) youth from the West Side. I had to choose my words incredibly carefully so not even a snippet of a quote would support that narrative—I basically didn't even answer the questions, I just said other things that were actually true—but it worked. When they played back the interview, there was nothing there about "getting into trouble," because I hadn't left him anything to work with. It built more trust with the kids—as soon as the reporter left, I realized one of the older, wiser young ladies had been watching intently, and she turned to me and said, "You're good at this." Again, these were our leader kids—she knew exactly what was happening there.
>
> Another time I was talking to someone running for local office about funding for school sports fields—our neighborhood middle school still does not have its own football field but shares one outside the neighborhood with other schools. The man told me, "People always say if we build a field here on the West Side, it'll just get torn up." I was taken aback, but gathered my wits and said, "What about our two community centers? Are they ever "torn up?" What about the new court that Cookie Miller (we met him in Chapter One) put in at Second Avenue? Has it been "torn up?" I realized in that moment that funding for a middle school field had been denied for years based partly on a narrative that the people in our neighborhood would trash it – a story that the bare facts didn't support. As soon as I told the story my way, the man saw my point, and realized the injustice in the fact that the idea had been shot down for so many years. How we tell stories about the communities we love is incredibly important, especially when

others are telling far less empowering stories about us and our neighbors.

It is important for a community to be able to tell its own stories, on its own terms. Timoteo Sports happened on a way of empowering their young people, both through empowering storytelling and through skills training, when they began incorporating a significant media component in their programming:

> About two years into my (Chris) Timoteo experience we had the idea to do "Timoteo TV." We began filming the games and getting post-game interviews from players and coaches and posting them on YouTube. Ten years later, media has become an essential part of Timoteo, as everything we do is posted on our websites, apps, and social media.
>
> Each year we upgraded our cameras and software until eventually each week became a production. Each week starts with Timoteo TV, as our Timoteo experts gather together every Tuesday night to talk about the upcoming matchups. Initially this show happened in my basement and consisted of a few random coaches each week—Today the show is filmed in the Timoteo building, and several youth and coaches show up to see what will possibly be said about them and what the Timoteo expert predictions will be. Through this experience we have been able to empower several youth through learning how to film, produce, and appear on the show. Initially most kids are pretty shy once the camera turns on, but over time our youth have learned how to articulate in front of a camera while keeping it interesting for the audience.
>
> The next part of Timoteo TV takes place on game day. Each game is filmed on an HD camera by youth that are paid to do so. Each cameraman is trained, and they quickly gain a skill that many pay attention to. Each game is filmed in its entirety and the film is used by coaches and players to scout for the next game. It is not unusual to have a team practice one time a week outside and one time inside, watching tape, and discussing strategy and game day verses, among other things. The use of media and the drive for excellence in our league has empowered youth in knowing how to be prepared for the opponent, while also being a reason to get together and build relationships.
>
> Another important aspect of our weekly programming has been creating Top Ten plays of the week. We did a sample top ten several years ago and it had so many hits on youtube we felt compelled to continue. Besides some amazing plays, each top ten has players dancing and performing for the camera, it is filled with

candid remarks from the sidelines, and much more. As the Top Ten rose in popularity we found that it was an empowering tool. We have heard stories of youth playing it for family members and later telling us they showed them because they wanted them to see they were good at something, as they did not receive praise at home. We have heard of teachers allowing some of our players to play the top ten for an entire class so they could see what they were able to accomplish on the field. We have seen folks with low self-esteem make the top ten, and it changed them and empowered them to try new things, even try out for high school football. At first, we thought having the games taped would be cool; we found out it has become an essential part of the ministry and an effective way of empowering our youth.

Just a few years ago we implemented "media school" as part of our summer camp. We were able to bring in someone who was an expert with the camera to teach some techniques, and then an expert on app development and editing. Each day our youth would learn something new, and they would then film the games in their entirety. Early the next morning they would edit the film and publish the tape, and each week they produced a Top Ten plays of the week. Not only have we added Top Tens to our weekly programming, but Timoteo youth can now gain a passion and skill for something they could make a living in. It is a dream to one day start a filming business that employs our youth to film and edit local projects. The potential is huge.

Empowerment is about the Holy Spirit bringing to life the gifts that are in each person in our community and including those people and their gifts in the solutions that allow the community to move forward. But for this to happen requires *leadership*—a central propelling force of Christian Community Development, and one that our sports programs are especially well-suited to produce.

Leadership Development: Building the Future

For neglected neighborhoods to transform into thriving communities, complex and interrelated problems must be met with creative, empowering solutions. Imagining and implementing these solutions requires skilled and courageous *leadership*, which is why *leadership development* is an important part of Christian Community Development.

Surgeons, singers, senators, and countless others whose careers have nothing to do with sports have pinned part of their success on the leadership they learned through athletics. Rock and Roll legend (and mediocre high school football player) Jon Bon Jovi drew on his sports experience to lead his band: "...you have to become a good coach, or you have to become a good quarterback, and you have to run the business the same way you would run a game" (Kilmeade, 2004, 86-87). Said former Senator and former Yale athlete John Kerry: "If you like sports and working out and trying hard like I did, it was quite a thrill if a coach walked up and said something encouraging to you. As an athlete, you live for times like that. You learn a lot about being a great motivator, because you learn what people respond to" (242).

But whether the field sits in the shadow of Yale's gothic towers or Cleveland's crumbling smokestacks, the opportunity to mold leaders through the game is the same. Every good coach knows that developing the leadership of certain players is essential to maintaining team cohesion and success. Research by Dr. Daniel Gould, faculty director of the Institute for the Study of Youth Sports (ISYS) at Michigan State University, suggests that the development of leadership, or as ISYS defines it, "a complex process that involves the effort of an individual (i.e., a leader) to help groups identify and achieve personal and group goals," does not happen automatically through sports participation, despite many believing that it does. Gould and Voelker write: "effective youth leadership development *requires* experiential learning. Young people in a leadership role need supervising adults to allow them to make 'meaningful' decisions and to become active agents in their own development," and conclude that "Of all the venues that may be used to develop leadership in young people, sport may be one of the most underutilized" (Gould & Voelker, 2010, 1-14).

The Leadership Void

As we work to empower and transform our distressed communities in North America, we often see a serious *leadership void*. In our highly mobile society, those from poor neighborhoods who gain access to opportunity and education have been told that success means "getting out," and many who might have offered leadership for their own communities have long since left for "greener pastures" in suburbs and other wealthier places. Many who are still in the community struggle to meet basic needs for themselves and their loved ones, and while a person from any economic background can certainly be a leader, it can be difficult for our neighbors to offer complex social leadership when most hours of the day are spent securing basic necessities. Failing education systems in poor neighborhoods fail to equip many young people with some of the tools necessary for social leadership, and systemic exclusion keeps some people from accessing positions of influence. Too often, young people with real leadership skills end up employing those skills from a young age to protect more vulnerable friends, provide for family members, or challenge the unjust systems they encounter, and are drawn into a cycle of violence, dependence, and punishment before they have a chance to apply their leadership in a positive way. The important task of developing the kind of leadership necessary to empower the community to solve complex problems requires patience, consistency, and courage.

The leadership development philosophy of Christian Community Development brings together several important values. Ultimately, because those who live in the community are best equipped to solve the community's problems, the best community leadership is grown up from within. This means that those of us who relocate to the community from elsewhere need to take special care to partner with those in the community to raise up these "indigenous," or native-grown, leaders. There is still a strong tendency in North America for those with opportunity to leave the neighborhoods they grew up in, but for the community to transform from the inside out, young leaders need to be encouraged, supported, and equipped to remain or return to reinvest in the community.

If we keep these values in mind, our sports programs offer us incredible opportunities to develop the kind of leadership in our young people that will empower them to help transform their communities. We are presiding over one of the best leadership development avenues available in our neighborhoods, and we may not even know it. Sports are an ever-present passion for our young people, and those of us who are mindful of our communities' need for strong leadership can seize this opportunity to build the qualities into our young people that will empower them to carry the community forward.

Developing Leaders Through the Game

One of the most obvious places for leadership development to take place is within the game itself. Dr. Don Hellison (1995), Professor of Kinesiology now retired from the University of Illinois at Chicago, developed a framework he called *Teaching Personal and Social Responsibility Through Physical Education*, which highlights the use of sports and physically active games to promote individual and corporate responsibility that can ultimately be applied to life outside the game. Hellison finds that for a program to succeed in developing responsibility, it must put the kids first (far too many programs seem to serve vicarious adult needs more than the needs of youth themselves) emphasize human decency (*competition* thrives in an environment of *sportsmanship*), and holistic self-development. Maintaining these environmental components is key to creating an environment that builds character and responsibility. In addition, the lessons are *embedded in the experience of the sport or activity itself*, drawn out through debriefing and self-reflection, and transferred into leadership skills (Hellison, 1995, 24-28).

Kerry Martin, Jr., a defensive back for the West Virginia University Mountaineers, played quarterback at Capital High School in Charleston, West Virginia, for four years. Kerry shares how his experience as a quarterback helped him develop skills that have translated into community leadership:

> On the field, being the quarterback, you have to know what's going on, how to put people in the right place. It's like an orchestra, everyone has their own instrument, everyone plays together, and when everybody plays together it makes the sound it's supposed to make. When everybody doesn't come together, you can hear it, everyone in the community will know.
>
> Leadership is about getting people to work together. I remember one game, it was our senior night, and our rival team was having a down year. We came out thinking we would blow them out. We ended up being down 28-14 at the half. We had to come together, stop the finger pointing and blaming, and get it fixed, and we won. I had to help that happen.
>
> It's the same principle for the community. People say they want to be successful—to be successful it has to be about more than just you. It's about succeeding together. To be a successful leader, you have to help make things grow, you have to help change people's perspective. When someone brings an opportunity to the table, people have to buy in. There's too much tearing each other down, too much blaming each other. We need to come together, unify.
>
> A lot of leadership is handling other people's mistakes. I know how it feels to make a mistake, how that pressure feels. A quarterback has to learn to handle people's feelings. When people don't come through, even though you might be mad at them, there's a certain way you have to talk to certain people. I let them know it's okay, nobody has a perfect game. Don't let it get to you. You'll have a mental breakdown if you let it get to you. You have to do the same thing to be a community leader. Leaders don't bash people, they tell them what's wrong and help them fix it.
>
> Being the quarterback of a successful team, you get a lot of public criticism. Sometimes the criticism is reasonable. It has helped me view different perspectives. I may have my perspective, but they have theirs and I need to listen. Sometimes it isn't reasonable. In those times you can either not respond or figure out a way to say what you want to say and still protect yourself. You are your own brand—you don't want to say something that will hinder you and hurt the feelings of someone else. It's helped me become more mature about the things I say, and the people I say them around. That experience has made it so much easier to lead in public on other things.

Now that I play college sports, it's a bigger fan base. I can be an icon, touch more people. But it also makes it easier to lead in my own community. I come back to the schools and talk to the kids, but it's really them knowing that I care for them, I want what's best for them, I wouldn't steer them in the wrong way.

I'm proud of one thing we did together as a community. When I was in high school, we lost a member of our community, Tyler, to gun violence. He was a great athlete and a great person. He had played football for South Charleston, a rival school in a suburb across the river, when South Charleston won back-to-back state championships. I was in elementary school and lived in a housing project in South Charleston then, and he was a mentor to me; he had a big impact on my life.

South Charleston was mourning that loss, and a lot of my close friends knew him or were related to him. We had a game against them coming up, and even though we were rivals, a lot of us were close with players on that team. We wanted to show our respect and mourn for Tyler, show we cared about how they were feeling. That's the thing with sports—it brings a lot of people together in times like that.

So, I put out a tweet, and talked to some people, asked everyone to wear black in honor of Tyler. South Charleston's colors are black and orange, while Capital's are blue and gray. That would mean Capital fans showing up in South Charleston's color.

And they did it! Our fans showed up in their colors. They made special shirts. I asked [our head coach] Carp if we could get Tyler's number, number five, on the back of our helmets. I kept mine all season. I can't find anyone who can tell me about a time that hometown fans showed up to a high school football game in their rival's colors. But we did it. We did it to come together as one community, to unify, to be stronger than violence. Leadership is getting people to work together, even when they normally wouldn't.

At Memphis Athletic Ministries, Coach Randy Odom and Coach Changa Cooper (whom we met in the last chapter) have found creative ways to draw out and develop the leadership of the young people on MAM teams. Randy explains how they have drawn on biblical concepts to invest in team leaders:

Think of it like this. My coach has a team of twelve to fifteen kids. But on that team of twelve, he's gonna find four to six that are his YLT (Youth Leadership Team), those are the kids that are committed. Jesus had Peter, James, and John, and then he had the twelve. He spent more time with Peter, James. and John, he invested in them heavily. Same thing. So those kids are the ones that are in the gym all the time, they're teachable, you can see that they want to grow. They're on the team, but my coach might do additional Bible study and discipleship with them, so he can make them leaders, and then they can impact the other kids.

We want to disciple them. A lot of times we disciple them to Christ. We have what we call a "Godly Game Plan," a three-month plan. Spiritually, physically, socially, how are they growing? So, they set goals, and we help them reach those goals, and hold to them. We want them to be the leaders and be able to reproduce themselves with other kids.

In addition to this leadership development strategy, MAM has found some unique ways to turn difficult situations that arise during practices and games into moments that model, draw out, and empower the leadership of the young people involved. Randy explains how "discipline" at MAM reinforces the standards of behavior, while at the same time building in young people a sense of mentorship, community, and responsibility for one another:

One thing we do, it's "with me." Let's say you [a kid] curse me out and you've gotta do twenty pushups. I [the coach] am gonna do them with you. The coach does the discipline, whatever the kid gotta do. Or he can say, you gotta do twenty pushups, I'm gonna do all of them for you, I'm gonna do fifteen, you only gonna do five. I didn't curse, why am I gonna do pushups? Well, what you do affects other people.

I've done this: "You know what? I'm gonna get these [pushups] for you. I didn't curse nobody out, but I'm gonna do them for you. Because you know what, that's what Jesus did. He didn't do nothing wrong—but he paid the price for you." It builds equity with the kid.

"It works, man." Coach Cooper elaborates. "That kid is gonna end up teaching other kids. There's nothing like seeing when you've got a team of kids, something happens on your team, one kid's gotta do discipline, and coach asks, 'Man, who's gonna take the heat for this guy?' And when you see a guy jump down there and do it, generally, you got another kid that's gonna get down, then another, and another."

MAM's approach draws on the principles of restorative justice we discussed in Chapter Three. By employing a form of discipline that allows coaches and young people to collaborate on a path forward, MAM coaches help their athletes develop both individual and collective responsibility for using their gifts together in a constructive way, fostering the kind of community leadership that will help develop creative solutions to difficult real-world situations.

Developing Leaders Through the Program

Much of the leadership development that takes place through sports happens as coaches and mentors help growing young leaders process and manage the complexities of the game. But we also have an enormous opportunity to develop leadership in our young people through the structure of our programs themselves. While some sports programs are essentially adult-run enterprises that deliver a "product" for youth, many successful community-development-oriented sports programs have found creative ways to incorporate young people into the process of running the program itself. Young people can develop leadership in our programs serving as youth or alumni coaches, creating media, serving in administrative roles, or performing any number of functions we delegate or design. In doing so, they can develop skills that will bolster their leadership capacity within the community now and in the future.

Timoteo's Davon Mandy first developed his leadership on the football field, later taking on other roles within the program, leading him to complete a college education and take up a leadership role within the community itself:

> One of my (Chris) fondest coaching moments was the time I moved from coaching a perennial playoff team to coaching a team that had about three or four wins in their entire history and had

never sniffed the playoffs. The team was full of athletes, but they rarely ever played as a team. I remember the first practice we did introductions. As everyone went around the circle mumbling their names I waited until the last guy stopped and I picked a random player to tell me everyone's name. He named a few, but ultimately failed at the task, so I had everyone run a lap around the monstrous field we were practicing at. I then had them gather again, and we repeated the process. Once again, they failed, and they ran. The third time, I gave them some time to really get to know each other's names. It didn't take long for everyone to know everyone on the team! To be a great team, it is not enough to be stacked with athletes. Those athletes need to function as a team, they need to know each other, and it is through these relationships that leadership is born.

On the defensive side of the ball it did not take long for Davon Mandy to step in as the leader. Few people have displayed the type of passion Davon Mandy brings to the table when it comes to football. Growing up in the Frankford neighborhood he was exposed to violence and activity no child should be exposed to. In 2008, as a twelve-year-old child, Davon found himself on a Timoteo field. Only hanging around for part of the season, Davon stepped away from the team and reemerged at the age of 16. I remember coaching Davon and quickly recognizing his passion and willingness to be coached. Seeing his passion and relentless desire to excel I had him play the ever-important rusher position (aka, the killer position). The killer position is an important one, as the rusher must get to the opposing team's quarterback and create disruption. To be an effective rusher you must have passion, and you must be willing to be a leader as the position is often the quarterback of the defense. Not only did Davon play the position well but he was able to grab the all-time Timoteo sack lead and he entered the Hall of Fame!

We interviewed Davon and asked him about the effect Timoteo had on his life. He informed us that the game had a huge effect, as it taught him accountability, the importance of depending on others and the importance of respect. Because we saw Davon's leadership qualities on the field, we hired him as one of the youth coaches for our Timoteo Summer Camp. He stressed that it was at the summer camp where he was given the tools to take his leadership to the next level. During the summer camp he was given the reigns to teach younger kids how to play football. But he also discovered that coaching on the field led to a growth in responsibility, and to relationships with the kids off the field.

Through coaching he got to know the kids well and he was able to coach them in areas of life other than football.

Davon emphasized the importance of the relationships he built on the field, extending off the field. In other words, multiplex mentoring was vital to real effective leadership. Leadership development can start on the field, but it never ends there. Davon talked about the vital relationships he built with those in Timoteo on and off the field, he has developed life-long friendships. He also credits the lessons he has learned on the field as giving him the confidence to be a leader in the classroom. Not only has Davon developed into one of the smartest players in Timoteo, he has become one of our premiere scholars, and he graduated from Lasalle University as one of the "Outstanding Graduates of the Criminal Justice Program for the class of 2019."

Growth Through the Gray Areas

Leadership development in distressed communities means seeing and developing strengths in kids who have often grown up in high-trauma, stressful environments. Some youth programs take their "hotshot" students, often from families who have groomed them for leadership, and make them leaders as students or recent alums, while the rest move on or fall off as they age out. But in our distressed communities, those with leadership capacity will often have complicated and confusing lives. Christian community leadership development is a long process, and it can be messy; we need to leave room for growth in "gray areas."

Depending on the environment, some young people with leadership potential can become tangled up in incredibly unhealthy systems and behaviors when they try to express their leadership too early, in an unhealthy environment. While selling drugs, engaging in fights and constantly challenging authority are all destructive behaviors, the strength-based thinking described in Chapter Seven can recognize that the motivations behind those behaviors often reveal leadership qualities. Young leaders who have been labeled disruptive or criminal or even incarcerated when they have stood up to systems that restrain and discriminate against them can be guided toward healthy activism. Those who fight to protect those they love can be empowered to protect the vulnerable in healthy and heroic ways. Those who turn to desperate measures to supply their needs can have their skills redirected toward positive enterprise. Leadership development in distressed communities often means accepting that those who can lead the community can have incredibly troubled pasts—sometimes *because* of their leadership gifts. We cannot let labels like *troublemaker, angry, dropout,* or *felon* blind us to the leadership gifts that God has placed in our young people.

Chris Lahr recalls an example from early in his time in Philadelphia:

> As mentioned earlier in the book, Timoteo often does things a little differently when it comes to doing God's work. Too often churches put too much emphasis on getting people to believe the right thing before allowing them to "do the work." We have discovered that by "doing the work," one often discovers who Jesus is, and their beliefs are altered. The greatest example of this is found in the passages of Scripture pointing to Jesus' gathering his disciples. In Mark we see Jesus approaching the brothers Simon and Andrew in chapter one and brothers James and John in chapter two. In both cases it seems they knew of Jesus, but they did not know Jesus. Instead of leading them in the sinner's prayer and having them sit through Kirk Cameron's evangelism class, he simply asked them to follow. The disciples were a diverse group of people ranging from fishermen to tax collectors to revolutionaries. James and John were known as the sons of thunder because of their anger issues (Mark 3:17), Simon, also called Peter, would later deny he even knew Jesus after hanging out with him for three years (Luke 22:54ff), and even after the resurrection was called out by the apostle Paul for being racially insensitive (Galatians 2:11ff). The disciples also included a tax collector, who was viewed as the bad guy, as they were typically people of Jewish descent who were helping the Romans oppress other Jewish people (Mark 2:15ff). Then there was Simon the Zealot (Luke 6:15), who was a part of a Jewish revolutionary group that used to kill tax collectors for fun on the weekends, and Thomas the doubter (John 20:24ff) and—oh yeah—Judas would sell Jesus out for a bag of coins, leading to his death (Luke 6:16ff). The disciples were a rag-tag group of mostly uneducated people (Acts 4:13) that were willing to follow and learn from Jesus. They had a desire to see a better life, and they saw Jesus as the way to that better life.
>
> My deepest regret was seeing one of our up-and-coming coaches be rejected by a local congregation. My first year as a Timoteo coach I developed a relationship with a youth that had leadership qualities all over him—I will call him Tyrell. He played before we had developed the Timoteo summer camp, so he never had the opportunity to coach the younger kids. That said, he was a captain for my team both years that he played for me. After high school he went off to college, and we didn't hear from him again until the following year as he came back because his girlfriend was pregnant, and he wanted to provide for her and the baby. It was great having Tyrell back in town, and we immediately made him

an assistant coach with our staff. He was very helpful, and his leadership shined as the kids looked up to him. The problem occurred in his third year when the coaching staff decided it was time to take a step back and allow Tyrell to become the head coach. The remainder of the staff would still be intact, they would still lead the weekly Bible studies, but we wanted to give Tyrell an opportunity to take his leadership to the next level.

Then the unthinkable occurred...the church sponsor decided to pull their support from the team because Tyrell was not a "born again believer" and they felt the head coach should be. They could not get over the fact that he was living with his girlfriend and was not attending church on a regular basis. What the church didn't know was that Tyrell did love Jesus, and did attend church when he could, but was limited in church attendance because he had to work on Sundays. They also didn't know that Tyrell grew up in a broken foster home and did not have a father in his life to raise him, or a healthy model of marriage to follow. Tyrell may not have been a choir boy, but he was faithful to his girlfriend, and he worked very hard at providing for his daughter and being a present father in her life. Sometimes following Jesus is not always black-and-white, right-and-wrong; sometimes Jesus leads us through gray areas.

When I think about Tyrell, I often think about the dinner Jesus had at Matthew's house in Mark 2:15ff (NLT). The passage tells us Matthew, the dreaded tax collector, invited Jesus over to visit with a group of "tax collectors and other disreputable sinners" (there were many people of this kind among Jesus' followers). But when the teachers of religious law who were the Pharisees saw him eating with tax collectors and other sinners, they asked his disciples, 'Why does he eat with such scum.'" Jesus went on to say he came for the sick and to call those who know they are sinners. Jesus embraced people in the gray. He walked with people where they were and showed them a better way. Jesus built relationships with those living on the margins of religious society and he empowered them to be leaders in this world.

By making Tyrell the head coach we would empower him with more responsibility in terms of running practices and game day management. We were not about to let him do it on his own – our philosophy is that coaching should always be done as a team, and our plan was to walk with him, lead the Bible studies, and make sure to mentor the players with their various needs. If the church could have had eyes to see, maybe they would have embraced Tyrell and invited him and his girlfriend to the couples' Bible study so that they could have a proper marriage modelled for them, and gain support in making such a move as marriage. Leadership development calls for action and reflection. Leaders become followers and allow the new generation to lead as the mentor helps the new leaders reflect on their action and make positive decisions going forward. The world is full of Tyrells, capable leaders from the neighborhood that have the tools and ability to lead in the community. The church needs to take note of Jesus' approach and embrace these leaders where they are, empower them as leaders, and model the way of Jesus for them as they move forward.

The kind of transformation that turns young people from struggling neighborhoods into community leaders takes years and demands incredible commitment and patience. The community leadership development process should ideally begin in middle school and run into early adulthood, and young people will need a consistent commitment from some of the same adults across this time. In many cases, after high school, a great deal of the "social safety net" will disappear for young people, including the daily meals, counseling services, and free opportunities to play sports and pursue other passions, and there will be a sense of disorganization among recently graduated peers who once shared a regular life together. Some committed social leaders will leave after high school for college or jobs, leaving yet another leadership vacuum, and their peers may or may not step up to fill the void. Budding leaders will need support through this whole process.

In West Virginia, the Midian Leadership Project has made a commitment to stay connected to young people as this process plays out. Midian begins offering support to students in middle school, through a local Fellowship of Christian Athletes group and a program that connects young football and basketball players to older athletes. In high school, Midian supports several teams by offering leadership development and by helping athletes achieve milestones along the way to adult success, such as drivers' licenses and standardized tests. Committed to staying in touch with students after graduation, the Midian Leadership Project organizes trips to college campuses where their graduates are studying and playing sports and offers leadership opportunities through sports and community service to those who stay in town. Sometimes new leaders emerge when those who led in high school leave for other places. Midian also stays connected with young people who are incarcerated or otherwise involved with the criminal justice system, or who spend time living with family away from town. The concept is that the future leaders of Charleston's West Side community have consistent support from their community network from the time they begin adolescence to the time that many of them emerge as the community's young adult leaders in their early-to mid-twenties; with the right support, their greatest challenges are converted to wisdom and strength, they receive the support that many from distressed communities need to complete college and other training, and they remain connected to their community if they spend time away, cultivating a "returner" mentality.

Leadership development in our distressed communities requires an intense and long-term commitment to sticking with our young people through pain and triumph, to seeing their value through God's lens instead of through the labels the world has projected on them, to enduring the heartbreak of failures and setbacks and to creating paths forward through challenges and opportunities. Developing our young people into the leaders who will transform our community takes skill and patience, but it produces some of the greatest joys of community development work.

Community Leadership Empowers Others

As leaders, we are always eager to share what we know. But in multicultural and under-resourced contexts, where solutions require creativity and flexibility, we need to be especially mindful of the need to empower the abilities of others, rather than replicate leaders like ourselves. We aren't called to make clones in our own image; we are called to call out the image of God in others. 1 Timothy 1:6-7 records Paul reminding his disciple Timothy: "For this reason I remind you to fan into flame the gift of God, which is in you through the laying on of my hands. For the Spirit God gave us does not make us timid, but gives us power, love and self-discipline." The Holy Spirit uses the influence of other Christians to awaken unique gifts in each person; it is part of an empowering leader's job to help bring those gifts to life.

In order to empower the leadership of others, we need to leave room for mistakes; our young friends will often make mistakes and, with help from their older mentors, learn from the opportunity to fix those mistakes and try again. Many of our young people will have been denied the opportunity to lead in other contexts and will have had very negative experiences with those in authority over them. We need to be ready for authority conflicts and growing pains as they know how to lead in a way that reflects the example of Christ.

Tony Dungy (2010), Super-Bowl-winning coach of the Indianapolis Colts and founder of the national nonprofit *All Pro Dad,* says in his book *The Mentor Leader*: "Mentor leaders create an environment in which others can be productive and excel. They set the parameters and guidelines for the task, project and continually recast the vision, and then provide the tools and equipment needed for everyone to be successful in their assignment and to ultimately accomplish their mission. In essence, they strive to furnish what is needed for the task – physically, mentally, emotionally, and spiritually

– and to accomplish the mission" (Dungy, 2010, 174). After years of applying the coaching philosophy that a leader's foremost job is to make others better and lift them up, Dungy defines empowerment this way: "preparation followed by appropriate freedom" (182). Community leadership, focused on the enormously complex mission of helping the community to create its own way forward, is focused on setting others up to succeed.

Community Leadership is Servant Leadership

Jesus Christ said to his disciples at the last supper, as recorded in Luke 22:25-27: "The kings of the [Nations] lord it over them; and those who exercise authority over them call themselves Benefactors. But you are not to be like that. Instead, the greatest among you should be like the youngest, and the one who rules like the one who serves. For who is greater, the one who is at the table or the one who serves? Is it not the one who is at the table? But I am among you as one who serves." Jesus showed us through his words, and through his example dying on the cross, that he wants us to treat those we lead the way he has treated us: by leading the way through example, self-sacrifice, and service.

At times a "scarcity mindset," the belief that there is not enough to go around, leads young people in our communities to believe that the only way "up" is on someone else's back, and that the only way to have something—even authority or influence—is to take it from someone else.

Jeff Thompson has seen this "scarcity mindset" at work, as young men compete for authority and influence, so 10:12 sports has worked hard to model Christ-like servant leadership:

> At 10:12, we work hard to create and sustain an environment where different aspects of who God created the young men to be are both celebrated and affirmed. The more secure they are in who God has made them to be, the less they feel the need to compete with one another.
>
> We reinforce servant leadership with the acronym M.A.S.S.:
> MODELING being the man that God has made you to be,
> ADVOCATING on behalf of others, especially those who can't advocate for themselves,
> SACRIFICING your desires for the benefit of someone else, and
> SERVING your brothers.

Whenever we see instances of servant leadership, we reinforce and celebrate those together.

Community Leadership is Courageous Leadership

To face difficult and painful challenges requires courage. 1 Corinthians 15:13-14 tells us, "Be on your guard; stand firm in the faith; be courageous; be strong. Do everything in love." Love—to put God first and to value other people in the same way we value ourselves, the bedrock of community building—demands enormous courage. The Lord told Joshua, as recorded in Joshua 1:9, "Have I not commanded you? Be strong and courageous. Do not be afraid; do not be discouraged, for the Lord your God will be with you wherever you go." Courage comes not from knowing the outcome, or confidence in our own skills or strength, but from knowing the Lord is with us.

Our sports programs are an excellent place for developing the kind of courage and boldness that makes for powerful community leadership. When our athletes are very young, courage might mean the willingness of a fun-sized running back to face a line of helmeted elementary schoolers and head for the end zone instead of turning back in tears. A few years later, courage might mean a quarterback continuing a drive after being sacked and listening to the hometown crowd jeer and criticize, or mustering the strength to talk to a coach about how to improve, or speaking up in the locker room to stave off a team meltdown. As they move toward adulthood, courage will begin to mean continuing to love those they care about, even when it means walking with them through difficult times. As our athletes grow in their ability to contribute to the team, they grow in their ability to offer courageous leadership.

Leading distressed communities forward requires taking risks, speaking the truth to power, and entering difficult places for the sake of the people we love. As we coach and mentor our athletes, we impart knowledge, wisdom, and skills to our young people as we help them grow—and when we help our young athletes cultivate *courage*, they develop the boldness to put those skills to work on the toughest challenges they will face.

Community Leadership Transforms Pain into Progress

Dr. Perkins writes: "Most effective leaders are the ones who recognize real pain, lead from within that pain, and lead the people out of their own pain. Of course, joy is a wonderful emotion and experience. God created joy, but it is not the starting place. Joy is a result or outcome... The leader who can tap into our pain and walk through it with us—bearing our burdens like Jesus bears them—is going to be a real leader" (Claiborne & Perkins, 2009, 45).

Many of the young people in our programs will come bearing the weight of individual and communal pain from their past and present experiences. For many of the reasons we have already discussed—the unique ability of physical activity to rewire the parts of the brain that deal with stress and trauma, the trust-building capacities of team sports, the comparative safety of the athletic experience among other failing systems—our programs can be invaluable places for our young people to engage with, transform, and heal their pain.

At times, we may find engaging with the pain that our young people bear to be overwhelming. Witnessing the strain that is placed on the tenderest souls of our community will break our hearts and tempt us to harden or withdraw. But in order to lead these young souls toward powerful leadership, we need to be able to engage in the process of transforming that pain into progress, something our sports programs are uniquely equipped to do.

With help from trusted mentors, it is those who have borne the pain of the community who are best equipped to offer the transformative leadership that will move the community forward. Those who have gone hungry know best the importance of keeping the community fed; those who have experienced or perpetrated violence know better than anyone the value of peace; those who have been incarcerated know firsthand the brokenness of our justice system, and what needs to change – *if* they are able to engage in the Christ-like work of transforming their pain into progress. By entering into the pain of our young athletes, and offering patience and support as they work their way through to the joy of transformation, we share in the amazing privilege of empowering them to one day lead the community through a transformation of its own, as they mobilize those around them to put their strengths to work transforming the community's areas of greatest challenge and pain.

Coming Together: A Conversation

What does it look like as young athletes grow into leaders who transform the community? And what role do sports play in that process? It's a marathon, not a sprint. In Charleston, West Virginia, I (Jeff) have had the joy of seeing a group of young athletes come together over time, putting their lives in the Lord's hands, finding strength in overcoming struggles, turning pain into progress, and empowering their friends along the way. We've dubbed four of them the "leaders of the free world:" Turan Rush, Dorian Etheridge, Leondre Rogers, and Calvin Wilder. By the time they were done "taking care of business" in high school, the graduation rate was up by 10% and a record number of their friends were off to college. But they can tell the story much better than I can:

Turan: Growing up in the West Side community came with good, and bad. The good part of it was everyone knowing each other and having people to lean on when they needed a helping hand. But the bad outweighed the good by far. Growing up in the West Side community would get wicked. Crime was the main source and what really kept everyone thriving. As a kid we was put in situations where we seen some of the worst things you could imagine, events a normal kid wouldn't even see in a movie. Rather it was prostitutes, people shooting up drugs, robbery, dead bodies, or police brutality. It's so easy to fall victim to the streets. Sports was one of main the reasons my friends and I wasn't accustomed to the crime life. My friends played football and basketball with the local teams in the community. From elementary school we was going to school together, and then to the same afterschool programs, and then to practice. We was hanging around each other even on the weekends, staying at each others' house.

Majority of us went to Stonewall Jackson Middle School. We was still playing football, and basketball under Coach Swayne who kept us in check and made sure we was doing good. Puberty was just kicking in and we was trying to find ourselves and who we wanted to be. Becoming a teenage boy you get curious and get into things. My friends and I didn't know if we wanted to be Pablo Escobar or Michael Jordan. It was so easy to become Pablo Escobar, because that's what we saw in the community and in our households. It was people in our life who already fell victim to the streets, and served prison terms. They was the ones telling us, "Lil homies! I promise prison isn't a place you want to be." At age 13-14, we was losing friends to jail for drugs and losing friends to gun violence. But the reason why because they was providing for their family. They had to put food on the table, pay the bills, and make sure their siblings had clothes to wear to school.

The transition to freshmen was scary at first, until we met Coach Carp, the head football coach. He told us--just do the right thing all the time and life will be smoove for you up here. Coach Carp knew the situations and backgrounds we surfaced from, so he understood us in ways a lot of people couldn't. He told our class to use football as a way to get out the situation we were in. Yeah, life was hard when we went home, but when we was at practice it was a totally different life. My friends and I used football as a way to escape the hardship of the life we was accustomed to.

With all the hardships in my life, God always found a way to put people in my life that was going to help achieve my goals and the people around me's goals. I met Jeff Biddle around my late middle school years. Jeff and I connected from Bible study on Wednesdays, and he helped me give my life to the Lord. Around the same time I got saved by our Great Heavenly Father. He was telling me—bring your friends around church, help them get saved. So I listened to Him. Before you know it, a lot of my friends was giving their life to the Lord. It wasn't an easy process for us, and will never be, but with the Great Lord's help it will be easier. Majority of my friends are saved. I can truly say with passion and honor that all of us want each other's dreams, goals and aspirations as much as we want them ourselves. When you have that in a friendship or brotherhood you have to have accountability. We held each other accountable for everything, even if it was something as small as raising the toilet seat to use the bathroom. None of us let each other lack at life because it would affect all of us. We would always be in each other's ear, saying, "You got this, don't give in." We told each other we had to make it in life so our kids wouldn't have struggle like we did growing up.

Dorian: I was one of those people Turan brought to church! My home life was good, but I wasn't close to God until then. I was always a vocal person, but leadership was thrown at me from a young age. I was forced to have to try to lead, 'cause I was more physically talented than others. Coach Carp would say that every day since I was fourteen. I embraced the role, you know, teams need leaders, so it was like—I guess I need to be one. But to be a true leader, there are so many aspects to it. My junior and senior year, it hit me. These guys, guys you would never think that you would care about, they're on the team just one year, and you just want the best for them. You make lifelong friendships playing football. That's what being on a team does for you. When that part came to me, to see people do better, and not just—oh, they need me to be a leader—that's when it came to me. God could call on me to be there for these people. Now that I'm playing at [The University of] Louisville, I'm in a leadership group, and I see the same thing. Some people lead 'cause they want to win. But when things are going wrong, guys always come to me and a couple other guys. The things I take the most pride in—the people who have been saved, the people who have changed. It's been a group effort. It's about giving people hope.

Calvin: I was never as good at football or basketball as any of these guys in the beginning! I got saved with my AAU coach one day after basketball practice. He was one of the people who also helped me get better at basketball. He used the sport I really liked, he got my trust that way. His son was also way better than me, and he would make sure I saw how his son would read a page of the Bible every day. I think he knew that when I saw that, I would want to do it. It worked. And I then I wanted to do it for other people. So I just started talking to people about it. When you're young like that and you hear someone your age talk about God, as opposed to an older person, you're going to want to learn more about it.

I started playing basketball at church with Turan, and started inviting people to church. I hung around people who was younger than me. I didn't do dumb stuff in high school, didn't smoke at all. I could be in a room with ten blunts and I'm telling them—I'm good. I guess people looked up to me. Soon I had a whole group of friends who liked basketball and shoes and Jesus. None of us were the best, none of us played for the school at first—except Leondre, who was known all over the state.

Leondre: I almost didn't play for the school! I got saved and baptized in tenth grade. But I had failed five classes that year, and I had to make them up before my eleventh grade year or I couldn't play. Once I did that for myself, I wanted to help my friends. We took care of business, made sure our work was never late, stayed eligible. Sometimes it meant spending our Saturday nights doing research. We made sure we were different from everybody else.

Turan: We took care of business for real! The results of having God in your life, a community surrounding you helping you get resources, and a group of friends that will push you to be great and hold you accountable — magic will happen. The graduation rate at Capital High School went up by ten percent when our class graduated. Most of that was our friends. My group of friends have more recent graduates in college and careers than Charleston had seen from our neighborhood in 30 years.

Calvin: At first I never thought about college. But I played for the high school my junior and senior year. I went to this team camp at a Baptist college, and I didn't have grades to go there right out of high school, and one of the coaches there suggested Potomac State Junior College, and they was able to get me there. The next year I got Leondre and our friend James to come to Potomac. I helped them and then they helped me. We took the school to number one in its division for the first time ever. Now, it's about succeeding together. All it takes is for one person to get their foot in the door. Then you can make relationships and bring people with you.

Turan: I was eligible but I didn't get the offers I wanted out of high school. So, I went to Antelope Valley Junior College all the way out in California. I slept on an air mattress, to remind myself it was temporary, not to get comfortable. By Christmas I had an offer from Eastern Michigan. It was countless people that was a part of our success, and was there to help us reach our dreams, goals, and aspirations. That's what community is for.

Dorian: Charleston ain't just a place for us. It's a part of us. It made us. Everything we know, the way we are, Charleston produced that. I love Charleston. I've got 304 (the area code for West Virginia) tatted on me. Turan has "Charleston" tattooed on his body. People say, I can't wait to get out of here, I can't wait to "make it." But your mentality is everything. If we bring positivity to Charleston, give people that little bit of hope, the city can be turned around. Other people at Louisville have one or two people back home. We've got a dozen or more that we keep in touch with every day.

Leondre: Coming from Charleston is bit of a challenge for some. Of course, there will be rainy days and stormy nights, but from what we've learned those are the situations that made us, because we stood strong through the difficulties. Mind over matter will go a long way! You can easily get influenced to do something negative, or you can be strong minded and rise above it all. My friends and I have been on a marathon that will soon come to a finish line of success, with life changing opportunities not only for us, but also our community. Sports have brought many important and influential people in my life that I am thankful for. They taught me many lessons and helped our friend group somehow put together a master plan to help everyone. The next step is to build businesses, to build wealth, to bring things here, to help the community come together.

Turan: When people think of sports, they think of who had scored this amount of points, who scored this touchdown or made a goal. Sports is more than that. Sports is a foundation for a brotherhood and sisterhood. Sports can really change people's lives. For my friends who played sports, we had the attitude and tenacity, this was our only way to get out of the circumstance we was in. We put 110% into letting sports take us to a more secure place in life. The beauty of sports is that it's so identical with life. Hard work, optimism, confidence, dedication, commitment, and time management. You need all that to live life without sports. Sports made me play for my brothers that were beside me. You didn't want to be the one not carrying the weight. Sports put people in my life that drove me to be the best version of me. All this includes my friends I grew up with that didn't play sports. What I want to do with my life and God-given talents—I want to return home. I want to be able to make certain every kid in the community has a chance and a platform to reach their dreams, goals, and aspirations.

Community leadership development is ultimately about preparing to pass the baton of leadership to those who have grown up within the community, and preparing them to receive it, something our sports programs are uniquely equipped to do. As their leaders, mentors, and coaches, we offer them the support necessary to overcome the obstacles they face and take up the transformative leadership that will move the community forward. To do this requires us not only to empower our athletes, but also to *advocate* for them—putting our own credibility on the line for the sake of their futures when the injustices of the world threaten to snuff out the transformational flame that burns inside them.

Advocacy: Standing Together

Former Chicago Cubs chaplain Noel Castellanos (2015) describes in his book *Where the Cross Meets the Street: What Happens to the Neighborhood When God is at the Center* how he came to faith after his football coach invited him to a YoungLife camp during his high school years in California, and how he followed God's calling into ministry in the diverse neighborhoods of the Bay Area. In his years as a YoungLife missionary, he developed a four-part description of the kind of effort required to minister to young people in diverse and economically challenging neighborhoods like the ones where he lived and worked.

Castellanos describes how such ministry begins with *proclamation and formation*, the evangelism and discipleship that lies at the core of most traditional church and parachurch ministries. Many of us who coach and mentor athletes are aware of many successful groups and resources that use sports to share the gospel and disciple young believers. Next comes the *demonstration of compassion*—when we see needs, we help to meet them, in a sense traditionally known as charity or relief or simply *giving*. Next comes *restoration and development*—the work of developing a community to a state in which it can stand on its own two feet. A great deal of what we have discussed in this book falls into this category.

But community development goes further—a ministry that seeks to invest in young people, raise up leaders, and empower the community, will not be effective without also considering how to remove what many call the "structural barriers" to the success of the community. "Structural" in this case does not mean physical but means the barriers to success that are based on the way the "rules" work—parts of the law and culture of wider society that prevent the community from succeeding. Castellanos calls this part of the work the *confrontation of injustice*.

As we enter into trusting relationships with young athletes and their families in our communities, as we listen to their stories and begin to partner in investing in their futures, we will quickly realize that there are repeated, ingrained injustices that are preventing the community from moving forward. Those of us who coach integrated sports teams may quickly realize that our athletes of color are being disciplined in school in much harsher ways than our white athletes. We may see families struggling to provide, not because parents are incapable of working, but because a felony conviction from earlier in life is making it nearly impossible to find a job or housing. We may see families with entirely justifiable legal claims—claims against landlords who refuse to do basic maintenance or claims to property that the city is trying to take for other purposes—ignored by municipalities and courts. We may see a child of immigrants wait years for a process of affirming his citizenship to play out successfully. We may try to help a young woman get an after-school job and realize in the process that the city's public transportation has bypassed her neighborhood, and that travel to most available jobs would take two hours or more.

When we realize that injustices are repeatedly blocking the progress of the people we love, we will have to deal with a range of emotions, including disappointment, anger, and the difficulty of adjusting our view of the world to accommodate what we see. At some times, there will be nothing that we can do besides walk together with our neighbors through the struggle, but at other times, we will decide we need to act in a public way. When we decide to act against injustice on behalf of those in our community, we enter into a type of ministry known as *advocacy*.

Empowering Advocacy

The Lord used the prophet Isaiah to tell his people that simply going through the motions or worship did not make them holy in Isaiah 1:13-14:

Stop bringing meaningless offerings!
    Your incense is detestable to me.
New Moons, Sabbaths and convocations—
    I cannot bear your worthless assemblies.
Your New Moon feasts and your appointed festivals
    I hate with all my being.
They have become a burden to me;
    I am weary of bearing them.

Isaiah instructed God's people in verses 16-17 that the forms of worship are meaningless without practicing justice within the community:

    Wash and make yourselves clean.
    Take your evil deeds out of my sight;
    Stop doing wrong.
Learn to do right; seek justice.
    Defend the oppressed.
Take up the cause of the fatherless;
    Plead the case of the widow.

Seek justice. Defend the oppressed. Take up the cause of the fatherless. Plead the case of the widow. For our life and worship to have meaning, we cannot turn a blind eye to those in the community who are being left behind, taken advantage of, and trampled on. Advocating for our community and its most vulnerable members is part of building the shalom, the wholistic peace, that God intends for His people as we live, work, and worship together. We cannot truly root ourselves in the community without responding to the needs of those around us.

Michelle Warren (2017), CCDA's director of advocacy and strategic engagement, says in her book, *The Power of Proximity: Moving Beyond Awareness to Action*:

> Proximity compels a response. Its transformative lens turns what we see and begin to understand into action. The action may not even be something we consider a choice because we are so intimately connected with those affected. We share their pain and are compelled to do something with what we have. (pg. 108)

Being rooted in the community creates proximity or closeness as we live alongside those who are unlike us in many ways, especially those in our distressed communities who have access to fewer resources. As we begin to understand what we see, we are compelled to respond with action.

Those of us who have greater resources—resources including not just money, but leadership and other skills, education, social connections, name recognition, and other things that make it easier to get things done—need to be willing to serve our community by advocating for those we love and live alongside. Just as we discussed in Chapter Seven, we need to learn to do this in a way that is empowering to the people we love and serve. We are not the savior or the hero, accomplishing ourselves what the community could not. Rather, we put our own resources to work to break down barriers and open up possibilities for the people of the community to take greater control of their own destiny.

The problems we see can be so many and so complex that it can be hard to know how to respond. At times, those of us who are accustomed to the system "working" may be quick to respond with indignation to an unjust event and feel compelled to act quickly and expect swift results, only to learn that the problem is far more complex and systemic. Other times, we may have grown so accustomed to something being wrong that we need a reminder that change is possible. Deciding when and how to act in a way that directly challenges unjust systems will require careful listening to the community, and prayerful reflection.

Advocacy can be personal—sometimes, the community needs to rally behind a single person whose situation needs support. This could mean vouching for a young person caught up in a criminal case, helping someone navigate a tangle of red tape to start a business, or organizing to push back when the city is trying to condemn a neighbor's house. We may do this by speaking directly to those in authority, or by offering to help with complex processes. Advocacy can also be systemic, which happens when the community organizes itself to advocate for change in large-scale systems. This could mean legal advocacy, such as attending meetings to lobby for better funding for the neighborhood school, finding advocates on the city council who will make sure green spaces are maintained or lots are zoned for new business, or organizing a ballot initiative for changes in the criminal justice system. This could also mean advocacy within the culture, using art, media, social media, and interpersonal relationships to change the perception of the community and its people or bring important issues to light. Advocacy happens anytime we use what influence we have or can create to remove barriers to progress and success and create new paths forward for the community. *Learn to do right. Seek justice. Defend the oppressed. Take up the cause of the fatherless. Plead the case of the widow.*

Sports and Racial Justice

In Chapter Three, we discussed the relationship between sports and racial reconciliation. Sports teams often create a proximity between young people and adults of different ethnic backgrounds. Unless we are intentional about how we handle this, these experiences will likely only reinforce the existing status quo. But if we choose to frame and use these experiences in a constructive way, sports can become a space of reconciliation, where people with differences learn to love one another and work together.

Racial reconciliation, however, is not the same thing as racial justice. Racial reconciliation involves people loving and understanding one another as neighbors and partners in God's mission. Racial justice means setting right things and systems right that have gone wrong in the past and that are still wrong now. When we become reconciled to one another, we lay the groundwork for taking action together, but change will not happen automatically; working for justice requires taking the next step into advocacy. For those of us who coach and mentor in distressed communities, this takes two primary forms: working to make sure that the dynamics of our sports teams and programs are just and taking our impact beyond our programs into the community as a whole.

Many racial dynamics of sports are obvious and much discussed. Several American professional sports (primarily those most popular in inner cities) continue to follow a pattern where a large number of the athletes are men and women of color, while nearly all the team owners, most of the coaches, and a large portion of the fan base are White. College level sports display similar patterns, and other than their scholarships, athletes are unpaid while colleges and associated industries bring in millions. This raises important questions about who is benefitting most, both socially and financially, from the current system, why Black and Brown people so seldom rise into the upper ranks of these industries, and how much the current racial dynamics of North America contribute to the disparities in these institutions. Dr. Beverly Tatum, an educational psychologist focusing on racial identity formation and the former president of Spelman College, defines racism as "a system of advantage based on race." Even when we cannot identify individuals responsible for causing specific harms, we need to be concerned about how systems are structured and who they benefit.

These issues are not limited to college and professional sports programs; similar racial dynamics play out in many of the school and community programs that feed the upper levels of North America's most popular sports, the very programs in which we coach and mentor. Proximity requires a response—as those with young people in our care, working within larger systems that often advantage other people, how do we respond well?

We all come from a certain social location and see the world in a certain way. We bring certain information, attitudes, and cultural knowledge to the table—and so do our neighbors. The key to empowering advocacy is to combine what we bring together and use our areas of influence to help everyone move forward. Jamie Jessup has seen both the upsides and the pitfalls inherent when social systems continue to bring middle-class coaches into contact with inner-city boys with athletic aspirations:

> Our social location and our experiences within those locations influence our understanding of those who are not like us. For example, a white male who grew up in Cheyenne, Wyoming, will have a perspective on Black America that's dissimilar to a Black male who grew up in a suburban context in Atlanta, Georgia. Because his interactions with Black youth were limited in Cheyenne, he would likely develop much of his understanding of Black youth culture from media and pop culture. He probably wasn't exposed to a curriculum which highlighted the systems of marginalization, injustice, and oppression which have set so many minorities back in America. He probably doesn't have much knowledge of the classroom-to-prison pipeline because children of color do not occupy the schools he attended. Instead, his curriculum is rooted in the depictions he sees from the news where Black men are either recognized for their athletic prowess or their

inability to avoid a life of crime. He understands the Black family to be incomplete because most many Black fathers shirk the responsibility of parenthood. He believes most Black mothers are physically incapable of raising Black boys into becoming men. He sees the Black boy as lost, in need of a savior; and if he only had the chance to reach and touch the life of this troubled soul, then all would be alright. He presupposes the messages in movies such as *Lean on Me*, *Freedom Writers*, *Dangerous Minds*, *Sunset Park*, *Coach Carter*, and *The Blind Side* are microcosms of Black culture and successful intervention to save Black lives. Herein lies the error in his judgment.

While well-intentioned, many leaders who take this approach actually cause more harm than good in terms of advancing the causes of marginalized youth. Leaders, whether they be male or female, Black or White, upper or lower class, who bring assumptions of minority culture absent of understanding ultimately approach these youth with an opinion from the social location with which they were raised. Coaches tend to approach these boys as orphans in need of a father figure: someone who can cultivate the talents within them. One of the most significant errors we made at the start of our ministry was the assumption that the young men we served lacked financial resources and consistent parenting. While that was true in some situations, it was not the case most of the time. Before coming to that knowledge, our approach was grounded in providing completely free resources and mentoring opportunities to all students in the program. Although we intended to affirm their dignity in Christ, we actually denied that worth, value, and talents by assuming they needed everything we had to offer. The question we had to ask ourselves was, who were we ultimately serving in the situation: the students or ourselves?

We must understand that we bring biases and assumptions into situations. These biases can be detrimental to the communities we serve. Additionally, we must realize we are nobody's savior. Instead, we are conduits by which God works through to bring about change in someone's life.

True advocacy requires us to listen and learn about our athletes, their circumstances, the community's culture—and the systems set up to benefit certain people. Good intentions are a good start, but as we begin to learn about the ways that many athletic programs are designed to benefit the school the program, the coaches, or the directors, at the expense of the athletes themselves, we can *serve* our athletes by advocating for *their* interests—and building our own programs to do so. This will ultimately require a wisdom and cultural knowledge that goes beyond our athletic programs themselves.

Racial Justice in the Community

The relationships that proximity allows us to develop within the games we love can also lay a foundation for pursuing justice beyond the sports world. In a diverse sports program, we have the chance to develop relationships with people of very different backgrounds, allowing us to deepen our understanding not only of our neighbors' lives, but also of the systems and issues that affect them.

In the spring of 2019, the NBA's Kyle Korver, former member of the Cleveland Cavaliers' back-to-back finals teams who now plays for the Utah Jazz, penned an article for the *Players Tribune* that he titled simply "Privileged." Both of Korver's parents played college basketball, and he grew up in mostly-Black Paramount, California, which borders Compton, and where his father was a pastor.

In his article, Korver reflected on how his long basketball career helped him grasp systemic issues as he grappled with specific incidents that affected his friends—when the NYPD broke his teammate Thabo Sefolosha's leg, or the tone of the media attention after fans publicly heckled teammate Russel Westbrook—and how he realized that while he cared about his teammates, he had the privilege of exiting such conversations any time he wanted to, which others did not. He felt compelled to respond:

> Maybe in years past, just realizing something would've felt like progress. But it's NOT years past — it's today. And I know I have to do better. So I'm trying to push myself further.
>
> I'm trying to ask myself what I should actually do.
>
> And I don't think I have all the answers yet — but here are the ones that are starting to ring the most true:
>
> I have to continue to educate myself on the history of racism in America. I have to listen. I'll say it again, because it's that important. I have to listen. I have to support leaders who see racial justice as fundamental — as something that's at the heart of nearly every major issue in our country today. And I have to support policies that do the same. I have to do my best to recognize when to get out of the way — in order to amplify the voices of marginalized groups that so often get lost.
>
> But maybe more than anything? I know that, as a white man, I have to hold my fellow white men accountable. We all have to hold each other accountable.

Korver's years of proximity allowed him to increasingly understand the needs and experiences of his teammates, and compelled him to use his public platform in whatever way he could to influence issues that, except for those relationships, would not have significantly affected him personally:

> I know I'm in a strange position, as one of the more recognized white players in the NBA...This feels like a moment to draw a line in the sand. I believe that what's happening to people of color in this country — right now, in 2019 — is wrong.
>
> The fact that black Americans are more than five times as likely to be incarcerated as white Americans *is wrong*. The fact that black Americans are more than twice as likely to live in poverty as white Americans *is wrong*. The fact that black unemployment rates nationally are double that of overall unemployment rates *is wrong*. The fact that black imprisonment rates for drug charges are almost six times higher nationally than white imprisonment rates for drug charges *is wrong*. The fact that black Americans own approximately one-tenth of the wealth that white Americans own *is wrong*.
>
> The fact that inequality is built so deeply into so many of our most trusted institutions is wrong. And I believe it's the responsibility of anyone on the privileged end of those inequalities to help make things right.
>
> So if you don't want to know anything about me, outside of basketball, then listen — I get it. But if you do want to know something? Know I believe that...
>
> And if you're claiming my name, or likeness, for your own cause, in any way...know that about me. Know that I believe this matters.

Unlike Kyle Korver, most of us do not have national platforms to speak from. But a great many of us have had experiences on sports teams that have deepened our understanding of what justice would mean for our communities and are grappling with how to respond.

Jeff Biddle talks about the way he has seen sports teams build awareness of racial dynamics that compel a response:

> When I was in my mid-twenties, I was working in a racially integrated youth ministry here in Charleston, West Virginia, and we were basically using sports as a way to stay grounded in relationships where adults could disciple young people. It was a great tool, but we quickly realized things were going to be more complicated than we thought. At the same time, I started doing

chaplain-style work with some local sports programs, just being there as a volunteer for moral support and encouragement.

I wanted to learn everything I could about how to help young people from tough backgrounds succeed. I started to see patterns, certain things happening over and over again, and I started to really understand what zero-tolerance discipline and the school-to-prison pipeline were doing to young people and their families. I started to see how different forms of discrimination were having this huge impact beyond just personal setbacks. Sports helped me realize those things, because there was such a contrast between the way we were treating each other on these teams, and the treatment that a lot of the young people were getting out in the wider world.

I started to ask myself, "How can it be that on a football team we invite these athletes to develop leadership, to hold each other accountable in their lives, to show creativity and strength, and we teach them to contribute and express their opinions with courage, and then send them into an environment where a Black kid who questions authority at all is immediately punished and maybe arrested? How is it that we hug these kids and tell them how much we love and value them, and then I wake up at two in the morning to a frantic phone call because, less than a block from my house, the police are holding those very same boys on their knees in handcuffs in the middle of the street, with guns to their heads? How can different people in our community see these kids so differently? How could our community ever be whole if things stay like this? How can all the leadership development and community building we are doing on our sports teams mean anything if it is cut down over and over again by other, bigger forces?" If we care about these kids, we have to actually do something, actually change things.

I watched the White kids, too. In our community they had most of the privilege, but when it came to their cross-cultural experiences their feelings were almost invisible. White kids were forming these life-altering bonds with Black and Brown teammates, and then watching those teammates get insulted, get expelled, get locked up, get taken away, go hungry—not all of them of course, but a slice of them—and they had no idea what to do with that. They had anger and confusion that it seemed like no one could see or help them with. And then there were the White kids that had similar problems, they were getting locked up, going hungry too—but seeing how much differently that was handled. People tended to think they were fine. Coaches, your White athletes with big hearts are not okay. Somebody needs to be talking them through their place in all this, and nobody is doing it.

There are lots of resources out there to help coaches and chaplains process some basic moral and faith questions. Athletes deal with specific issues around identity – "Who am I outside this sport?" And there are lots of resources to help athletes and coaches connect their sport with their faith. But in my chaplain-style roles, I was hearing more and more that coaches were wanting to understand and handle the big social issues they saw affecting their athletes. They can't compartmentalize that stuff away. I really believe most coaches care deeply about the young people they coach. They're certainly not in it for the money! But coaches of all backgrounds are struggling to understand these big undercurrents in education and recruiting and criminal justice and interpersonal cultural conflict, that affect their athletes' everyday lives and their team dynamic. If there's anything that sports chaplains need to be offering moral support and encouragement about, it seems to me that's it.

It's clear that sports are doing something important. It's funny to me how over and over again if I'm in public with Black young people, or even Black friends my age—people assume it's because of sports. People assume we are some kind of team, even if we aren't. I go to a multicultural church and live on a multicultural block. I might have a few of the neighbors' kids or some folks from church with me, but people ask, "Are you their coach?" or even just "Did y'all win today?" It's clear that people see sports bringing unlikely people together. But at the same time, it annoys me a little that people don't see it as deeper than that—as if we can only come together to win a game. The number two assumption people seem to make about mixed-race groups, especially if we are dressed down, is that it's about drugs. One time a Black basketball coach was driving, and I was in the passenger seat, and we passed the security shack at one of the housing projects, dropping off a kid. I had passed this checkpoint plenty of times for the same reason, but with the Black coach in the driver's seat and me with him, the guard started grilling him about what he was doing there, and even—you can't make this stuff up—asking how it was that he has such a "nice car." He handled it great, but I was speechless. How do you explain what just happened to the athletes in the back seat? They see and hear that stuff. They wonder what it means. Another time two young adult Black men from church stopped to talk to me through the window of their car a few blocks from my house. It turned into a forty-five-minute stop-and-search by some nearby cops, as though just our being together at all was "suspicious." We have to learn to use sports as a starting point, a place to work from to get to the point that us being together seems normal to everyone. But we have to help people understand that while sports is a starting point, Jesus makes it work.

I want people to know that football and Jesus is enough. If you play football or basketball or any sport that gives you a brotherhood or sisterhood with people of different backgrounds, and you've got the love of Jesus in your life, you've got the Bible to tell you about the kind of peace that God envisions for everyone together—it's enough. Keep going. Keep trying to understand. It's enough to awaken you to the reality of the work we need to do, together, on behalf of one another, to make things right. You don't have to be a trained activist or an academic or have some sort of crazy life story like Kyle Korver. Once upon a time, Kyle Korver was just a White pastor's kid on a mostly Black basketball team. Basketball and Jesus, Football and Jesus, whatever it is for you – it's enough to bring us together and get us started. Your hometown team, with Black kids and White kids and Latinx kids and Asian kids, or whatever backgrounds they have, playing together, building a life-defining bond as they grow together, if you've got the love of Jesus in it, you've got enough to get you started to really change the community. I'm not saying you won't need help along the way—I went searching everywhere for all the help I could get once I realized what I was seeing. But it's enough. It's enough to realize the truth about some really hard things and start moving forward.

On our sports teams we build these incredible bonds. 250-pound linebackers who could tear apart pipes with their bare hands cry and cling to their teammates when the season is over. We call our teammates our brothers and sisters. We say we would do anything for them. We'd better mean it. We learn things about each other that few people know. How are you going to steward that knowledge? We'd better use what we've got to help us all move forward together. It takes a lot of courage to tell the truth about what we see, and it takes a lot of wisdom to listen well and learn to work together. But if we are the brothers and sisters we say we are, then we had better get to work.

What does it look like to advocate for one another beyond the sports world? Advocacy takes many forms. For Jon Carpenter, the football coach at Capital High School where many of Jeff Biddle's students play, it meant going to bat for students whose futures were endangered by the systems they faced. Jon's story is another perspective on the leadership story we heard in Chapter Eight. As young leaders were coming into their own, their coach was advocating for them behind the scenes:

> I grew up in Cabin Creek, West Virginia. My dad worked in the coal mines. Every boy I knew thought he would be a coal miner. My parents divorced when I was in middle school, and football was the only thing I had that gave me people to be around, something to escape to, something to be part of. I didn't have dreams of going to college—I had dreams of being a teacher, the only thing that was gonna keep me from working 180 feet underground. I went to college and started coaching high school football before I graduated.
>
> I got hired as an assistant at Capital High School, then as head coach. My wife and I ended up adopting two little girls from the Caribbean. The adoption process is tough, absolutely crazy, and at the time we wanted to adopt, that was the door God opened. Looking back, I think about how God sent me two little Black girls, He had a plan. I get a daily reminder of how unfair the world is to people. He made sure I was completely invested. When it's your own kids, you gotta be willing to fight every day, 'cause you'd want someone to fight for yours.
>
> My third year of coaching, we only had five seniors on the whole team. The others had dropped out of school or been kicked out. A lot of the kids on the team, their dads had been kicked out of Capital, thrown out on the street during the first big purge (Jon is referring to the first "zero tolerance" school discipline push in the late 1990s and early 2000s). They felt like, "Sure as rain, that's gonna happen to me too. They'll get me one way or another." It's sad that this was their outlook, but that's the way it was for them.
>
> There's still this "slaveowner" mentality in the schools. They think if they whip the biggest one, everyone else will be so scared that they will fall in line. It happens every year. If the football team has been good, the star football player is the most famous guy here in the first months of school, and if that kid comes from the wrong side of the tracks, life is hard for him. He's targeted, he's humiliated, to keep the others in line. Everyone wants a piece of him—teachers, principals. 95% of the conversations at school about my best leaders on the football team are negative. A lot of these are Christian kids, kids with good grades, but the attitude towards them is—whip these ones to keep the others in line. They're cutting down the leadership instead of nurturing it.
>
> It's not about whether they did anything wrong—it's about asserting power. It's a Jim Crow thing, still. And these are kids.

Even when they're in a situation where they need help, somebody asserts power over them. Even when they're right, nothing's harmonious. People in authority challenge them over and over again, act like they're about to turn into some monster. It's every day. Fifteen-year-olds. Someone is always trying to keep them in check, instead of nurturing them, protecting them, educating them. These kids aren't afforded the opportunity to explain themselves, to have things explained. It goes from zero to 100. Even the compliments sound like: "You should say thanks to me for allowing you to have this." That's that Jim Crow mentality. For me these kids are the best leaders, but other people over them don't want any of them to become too powerful. And if the boys don't go along with it, if they get upset when it happens, they get punished, kicked out of school, maybe even taken out in handcuffs. It means losing their diploma, losing their football career, losing their chance at college. Over the smallest things, how they walk down the hall, having a cell phone in their hands. You'd be shocked, for all the talk about raising graduation rates, how quick people are to take that away.

You try to explain this stuff—how they are challenged every day by adults, by teachers, by people who work in the Go-Mart. The way I was raised White people don't ever know these things, they think it's not a big deal. But it is a big deal. I've realized it's harder for me to put up with, as a White man, because It's like a constant ringing noise in your ears, and my Black friends learned years ago to tune it out most of the time. I can't tune it out.

The principal who hired me, he's retired now. He was Black. He brought me in his office one day, and the first thing he said to me was, "No one is ever going to say you're a good coach." I said I didn't care, and he said, "I know you don't." Then he showed me newspaper headlines, "Capital outruns opponent," "Capital's athleticism..." Every story about the kids' physical abilities, nothing about teamwork or coaching or leadership. I had just spoken my mind to the press and the school board a couple weeks ago, and—I'll never forget this—he brushed his own brown skin, and looked at me, and said, "This is who you are now, to them." He was trying to tell me about White privilege, but that word wasn't being thrown around then. He was trying to tell me how people would see me, once I decided to take up for these kids.

When they brought those dogs to the state championships—I think about that every day. They made me choose that day. Am I gonna distance myself from the kids I coach, or am I gonna tell the truth about what I've seen? You gotta choose whether you're gonna please the people downtown or stand up for these kids. I told the truth. Do you know how much more difficult that made my life? As soon as I said what I said that day, I knew I was gonna be on the outside.

But I had already made up my mind. We were gonna be there for them, protect them. We surrounded them with people that loved them, Black, White, men, women—people who would stand up for them. Some of these guys don't have anyone in their corner. Trying to explain the stuff that happens to them. It's like a UFO landing in your yard. You don't tell the world. They won't believe you. But you call a few people you trust, to see if you are really seeing what you think you see and ask for help. So the people we surrounded our team with—it was a coalition of the willing. Certain people in the community would come together to back the kid up. 90% of the stuff they were losing their futures over, people will back off if they know someone's watching, someone's in the kid's corner.

And it worked. We haven't lost one to the system in four years. All most of them needed was a fair chance, and they could do what they needed to do. But we had to go to bat for them. The community came together, backed these guys up, and they ran with it, and now we've got more in college, more in jobs, more young leaders in our community than we've seen in years.

People say "Oh, you just want to win—you don't want the kid to be ineligible." or "Why don't you go to bat for the ones who don't play football?" The truth is, we go to bat for them whether they're a star or sit on the sidelines—that's community. Young people are supposed to have a support network. We do what we can for the people we have a connection with.

Turan was the spiritual leader of our team. Turan and Dorian, (whom we met in the last chapter) they had a lot of faith. I always thought God protected them. The other kids knew they would be there for them. But their ability to play Division One football protected them, too. Even the people who held them back along the way want a picture with them now. But there are plenty of kids who aren't going to play college football. They don't have that protecting them. They need us too.

You hate to say it, but once I've spoken out about these things, I can be the winningest coach, but—a lot of trouble comes your way, a lot of people want to bring you down, 'cause you're upsetting a system that works for their benefit, and you lose a lot of friends.

It's the right thing to do, though. There was never a cognitive decision to weight the outcome, just the right thing to do.

In Charleston, advocacy meant standing up for kids who were being discarded by the system. This is a common issue, but in other places, it may look very different; it all depends on the needs, culture, and structure of the community. As we mentioned in Chapter One, the proximity created by our sports programs leads to personal transformation, as athletes from the shooting guard at your local high school to Kyle Korver can attest. But to bring this new understanding to bear on the community as a whole is a long and complex journey. White athletes who have found brotherhood with athletes of color will likely need a certain shepherding to learn to handle this new reality with grace, and learn what to do when tense racialized situations emerge, or they experience disbelief and rejection from others they are close to who have not shared their experiences. The disproportionate number of white coaches who coach athletes of color in the United States will need to work hard to steward their authority well. For Christians in community development, Daniel Hill's (2017) *White Awake* and Michelle Warren's (2017) *The Power of Proximity* are starting places.

Sports and Educational Justice

In North America, sports and education are closely linked; many of the most significant opportunities our young people have to play sports are offered and funded by schools and colleges, and in turn, many successful athletes pay for their college education through highly competitive athletic scholarships to college. In turn, this means that sports programs based in educational institutions are closely linked to the ongoing issues of education equity in North American schools. Jon Carpenter's story is one example of sports empowering people to engage in issues of education equity; a quick survey of the landscape of sports and education reveals many continuing issues at play.

Dr. Earl Smith (2014), in his book *Race, Sport, and the American Dream* documents the tenuous connections between athletic recruiting and actual academic success—for instance, at the time of his writing, nearly half of all bowl-bound teams in the NCAA ultimately graduated less than 50% of their African-American football players (107). Many colleges push athletes toward classes that are easy to pass, but carry little workforce value (111-113). Dr. Richard Lapchick's Institute for Diversity and Ethics in Sport at the University of Central Florida keeps yearly statistics on sports participation and graduation rates for college athletes, which consistently reflect a wide disparity in outcomes for different groups at different college programs.

Anyone who has spent time around the college recruiting process, especially in inner-city neighborhoods, knows that while some real and important opportunities are created through athletic scholarships, the landscape is littered with false promises designed to take advantage of and profit from the dreams of our young people. Schools, coaches, "agents," AAU programs, and countless other actors lure young people to their teams and programs with unrealistic promises and varying motivations.

Teaching and coaching in public schools and running a college access program, Jamie Jessup has learned to look for the brokers and revenue streams that shape the "offers" and promises made to our athletes:

> There are many colleges, camps, AAU programs, prep schools, and personal trainers throughout the country willing to offer services to our most talented athletes who exhibit exceptional potential on the court or field of play. These organizations pour a plethora of resources into these players, preaching a message of support and love. Many of these players endorse these organizations because they were given a chance that so many other youth never receive. However, if we were to explore these scenarios further, it would appear as if the greatest beneficiaries of these programs are those who run them. Often, the highest-paid employees of the state are the head basketball and football coaches of universities receiving millions of dollars per year from endorsements while the players receive a year-to-year scholarship to cover tuition and meals. AAU programs sponsor their top players by providing free shoes, clothes, and travel, but frequently head coaches receive paychecks from large shoe companies to point their most talented players in the direction of the schools these shoe companies are contracted with, sometimes receiving far more than the athletes ever do. While one may argue these athletes have been allowed the opportunity to "come up" out of their difficult situations, many fail to graduate, "go pro," or receive the promise of that scholarship.
>
> Additionally, while these youth pour the energy and strength of their high school and college years into these programs, very little is done in this process that improves the communities from which they come. Primarily, the message is sent that your worth and value comes from your talents and not the community which developed them in their early years. Ultimately, the coaches, schools, and programs are viewed as the "savior." The institutions become reliant on youth who fit the description of "underserved" to serve their purposes, knowing that misguided perception fuels their success. The reality is we as leaders of youth must be willing to engage ourselves in a "cultural curriculum" of the communities we serve. There is not a cookie cutter approach to the

beforementioned suggestion. It is incumbent upon all of us who work with youth to engage in the practice of listening and learning before we act. We must speak with community leaders, teachers, principals, coaches, youth workers, and parents to determine who it is we serve, and how we can best serve them.

To successfully navigate this complex terrain, our athletes need true advocates, people who keep only their best interests in mind and walk them through these processes. One of the most important things we can do for our athletes is to help them be realistic about who they can trust, and how these processes really play out.

Advocacy happens any time we confront the injustices of the structures that exist in order to create better paths forward for the community and its people. Advocacy is challenging; to find the right empowering posture with which to come alongside our neighbors, to amplify one another's voices without drowning anyone out, to organize ourselves to make real changes in the structure of the community, is far more of an art than a science. It requires patience and listening and accountability. But if we can stand together on the field as a team, we can stand together in the community as God's people.

Conclusion

And now these three remain: faith, hope and love. But the greatest of these is love.
– 1 Corinthians 13:13

FAITH. It takes faith to believe that we have the power to change things, but Jesus told us that faith as small as a mustard seed could move a mountain. *I can do all things through Christ who strengthens me* is more than an inspirational pregame Bible verse--*all things* means the hardest things, the deepest things, the most challenging things, the most important things. It takes enormous faith to commit to weathering the struggles and joys and cares of a community for years on end. But with our faith in Christ, we can persevere through the deepest and most challenging aspects of our calling. *Keep believing.*

HOPE. Hope gives fuel to our visions. Hope shows us what is possible. Hope paints a picture of *shalom*, an image of joy and peace on the faces of our friends and neighbors. When sports focus our energy and channel our joy they give us *hope*--a taste of what can be, a glimpse of what is within reach. If you have ever shared the thrill of a hard-fought victory with your teammates and thought, *this has to be more than just a game,* if you have ever known the joy of watching young athletes come into their own and thought, *these people could change the world*, if you have ever sat amid a sea of thousands of faces wearing the same colors and cheering at the same moments and thought *this unity doesn't have to end here,* you were right. Those stirring feelings are *hope. Chase that feeling.*

LOVE. The greatest of these is love. It is love that fuels our passion: love for the game, love for our teammates, love for the athletes we coach, love for our community, love for our neighbors, love for the Lord. When we are at our best, love is why we keep playing our games--we love to play, we love who we play with, and we love what the games bring out in us and in each other. And love is why we keep working for a brighter future for our community, because we love the Lord, we love our neighbors, and we love the place we call *home.*

Keep the Faith. Persevere in Hope. Do everything in Love. Keep playing for the city.

References:

Ayers, W. (2001). *Zero Tolerance: Resisting the Drive for Punishment in Our Schools.* New York: The New Press.

Alexander, M. (2012). *The New Jim Crow.* New York: The New Press.

Bradshaw, B. (1993). *Bringing the Gap: Evangelism, Development, and Shalom.* Monrovia, CA: MARC Publications.

Brendtro, L. & Larson, S. (2006). *The Resilience Revolution: Discovering Strengths in Challenging Kids.* Bloomington, IN: Solution Tree Press.

Brooks, S.N. (2008). Fighting Like a Ballplayer: Basketball as a Strategy Against Social Disorganization, In E. Anderson (Ed.), *Against the Wall: Poor, Young, Black, and Male* (pp. 147-164). Philadelphia: University of Pennsylvania Press.

Castellanos, N. (2015). *Where the Cross Meets the Street: What Happens to the Neighborhood When God is at the Center.* Downers Grove, IL: InterVarsity Press.

Claiborne, S. & Perkins, J.M. (2009). *Follow Me to Freedom: Leading and Following As An Ordinary Radical.* Ventura, CA: Regal Books.

Connor, S. (2002). *Sports Outreach: Principles and Practice for Successful Sports Ministry.* Fearn, UK: Christian Focus Publications.

Duke, J. & Bonham, C. (2013). *3D Coach: Capturing the Heart Behind the Jersey*. Grand Rapids, MI: Revell.

Dungy, T. (2010). *The Mentor Leader.* Carol Stream, IL: Tyndale House Publishers.

Ehrmann, J. (2011). *InsideOut Coaching: How Sports Can Transform Lives.* New York: Simon & Schuster.

Fujimura, M. (2017). *Culture Care: Reconnecting with Beauty for Our Common Life.* Downers Grove, IL: InterVarsity Press.

Gluckman, M. (1955). *Custom and Conflict in Africa.* Oxford, UK: Basil Blackwell Publishing.

Gordon, W. (1995). *Real Hope in Chicago.* Grand Rapids, MI: Zondervan.

Gordon, W. & Perkins, J.M. (2013). *Making Neighborhoods Whole: A Handbook for Christian Community Development.* Downers Grove, IL: InterVarsity Press.

Gould, D. & Voelker, D.K. (2010). Youth Sport Leadership Development: Leveraging the Sports Captaincy Experience. *Journal of Sport Psychology in Action,* 1(1), 1-14.

Hellison, D. (1995). *Teaching Responsibility through Physical Activity.* Champaign, IL: Human Kinetics Publishers.

Hill, D. (2017). *White Awake.* Downers Grove, IL: InterVarsity Press.

Kilmeade, Brian. (2004). *The Games Do Count: America's Best and Brightest on the Power of Sports.* New York: Regan Books.

Korver, K. (2019). Privileged. *Player's Tribune.* Retrieved from https://www.theplayerstribune.com/en-us/articles/kyle-korver-utah-jazz-nba

McNeil, B.S. (2015). *Roadmap to Reconciliation.* Downers Grove, IL: InterVarsity Press.

Perkins, J.M. (1976). *Let Justice Roll Down.* Ventura, CA: Regal Books.

Perkins, J.M. (2007). *With Justice for All* (Third ed.). Ventura, CA: Regal Books.

Pohl, C.D. (1999). *Making Room: Recovering Hospitality, as a Christian Tradition.* Grand Rapids, MI: Eerdmans Publishing Company.

Powell, K., Griffin, B., & Crawford, C.A. (2011). *Sticky Faith: Youth Worker Edition.* Grand Rapids: Zondervan.

Rah, S. (2010). *Many Colors: Cultural Intelligence for a Changing Church.* Chicago: Moody Publishers.

Ratey, J. (2008). *Spark: The Revolutionary New Science of Exercise and the Brain.* New York: Little, Brown, & Co.

Rios, V. (2011). *Punished: Policing the Lives of Black and Latino Boys.* New York: New York University Press.

Smith, E. (2014). *Race, Sport, and the American Dream.* Durham, NC: Carolina Academic Press.

Stevenson, H. (2003). *Playing with Anger: Teaching Coping Skills to African American Boys through Athletics and Culture.* Westport, CT: Praeger Publishers.

Warren, M. (2017). *The Power of Proximity: Moving Beyond Awareness to Action.* Downers Grove, IL: InterVarsity Press.

Weinberg, R., & Gould, D. (2007). *Foundations of Sports Psychology* (Fourth ed.). Champaign, IL: Human Kinetics.

Zehr, H. (2015). *Changing Lenses: Restorative Justice for Our Times.* Harrisonburg, VA: Herald Press.

Acknowledgements

We would like to thank the Up2Us Sports Network, The Emerald Youth Foundation, Memphis Athletic Ministries, Bloc Ministries, New Level Sports Ministries, 10:12 Sports, Timoteo Sports, Camp Clutch, and the Midian Leadership Project for contributing time, experience and material to this book.

We would like to thank Dr. John Perkins and the Christian Community Development Association for their decades of spiritual, intellectual, social and emotional support of ministries in communities like ours. We would especially like to thank Lisa Rodriguez Watson for her leadership and support in making this book possible.

We would like to thank Urban Loft Publishers, especially our editor, Dr. Kendi Howells Douglas, who walked us through this process with incredible encouragement and wisdom.

We would like to thank our families for their continuous love and support throughout this process.

We would like to offer deep gratitude to the hundreds of young athletes embedded in our communities whose faith, dreams, perseverance, drive, loyalty, and love are an inspiring picture of our collective future that drives our daily work. This book is for you.

Most of all, we want to thank God through our Lord and Savior Jesus Christ. To Him be the glory.

JAMES "JAMIE" JESSUP
is founder and director of Camp Clutch basketball program in Winston-Salem, North Carolina. In addition to coaching, Jamie serves as a middle school and high school teacher. Jamie currently resides in Atlanta, Georgia with his wife and family where he still coaches high school football and basketball.

CHRIS LAHR
was the General Manager for Timoteo Sports in Philadelphia for over a decade. He currently lives in Fort Wayne, Indiana, where his wife works as a midwife, and he applies his lifelong passion for working with youth as a skills coach for the Bowen Center. He has an MDiv from Asbury Theological Seminary and did his undergrad at Eastern University.

JEFF THOMPSON
is the founding director of Baltimore's 10:12 Sports, and previously founded and taught at Urban Promise Academy Delaware. He is a graduate of the University of Delaware, where he was a Division One scholarship football player.

REV. DR. JEFF BIDDLE, JR.
is the founding director of the Midian Leadership Project, a sports-based community development nonprofit based in Charleston, WV. He earned his BA in economics from Harvard College, his M.Div from Trinity Evangelical Divinity School, and his D.Min from Palmer Theological Seminary, where his thesis focused on the use of sports as a leadership development tool for boys affected by the school-to-prison pipeline.

Made in the USA
San Bernardino, CA
10 August 2020

76283955R00110